Praise for Alicia Cahalane Lewis

Alicia is a gifted, loving, and compassionate healer. She has been an integral part of my spiritual awakening in this healing journey. I am blessed to know and work with her.
—Dawn Omo, Reiki client

Alicia is kind, compassionate, and nonjudgmental in the way she creates and holds space for your process, while gently guiding with a grace and a light that is subtle and powerful. The meditation series is simple and accessible, coaching you on connecting to your self, the Earth and the cosmos in a way that becomes foundational. Wherever you are those visuals come to aid when called upon. I'm grateful to Alicia for being a kind and wise teacher to me. I have learned a lot from her, and admire her grace and the way she expresses the etheric in a tangible way.
—Madi Omo, Reiki client

Alicia takes great care to translate the seemingly hidden language of healing modality to words accessible for human development. In this work, consciously and subconsciously, the meditative text allows for self-development through gentle and powerful push and pull of "spirit."

—Tiernan Ryden, Reiki client

I first met Alicia at a spiritual conference in Laguna Beach back in 2003. I first noticed her professionalism, her poise, and the classy way she presented. When we first spoke, what instantly struck me was her deep inner strength and overarching humility. Of all those present in that room, I knew that she was a true healer. Alicia is a person with the utmost of integrity. She is guided by virtue, morals, and values, and she is passionate about her profession. I am fortunate and feel blessed to be able to call Alicia a colleague and a friend.

— Dr. Dave Ferruolo, LifeWorks Counseling Associates, PLLC, Forever Frogmen Foundation

Alicia Cahalane Lewis

THE INTREPID MEDITATOR

ALICIA CAHALANE LEWIS is a ninth generation Quaker from the Shenandoah Valley of Virginia. She holds a MFA in creative writing from Naropa University where her poetry appeared in Not Enough Night. She is the author of *nebulous beginnings and strings* featuring art by Winslow McCagg. Her chapbook, *The Fish Turned the Waters Over So The Birds Would Have A Sky*, a contemplative meditation on the origins of evolution, was published by The Lune Chapbook Series. A Reiki Master of Masters, Alicia continues to live and work in the Shenandoah Valley.

aliciacahalanelewis.com

THE INTREPID MEDITATOR

The Intrepid Meditator

CONNECTING SOUL TO SELF

Alicia Cahalane Lewis

Tattered Script Publishing

Tattered Script Publishing
PO Box 1704
Middleburg, Virginia 20117
tatteredscript.com

Copyright © 2021 by Alicia Cahalane Lewis

Tattered Script Publishing LLC supports copyright. Thank you for supporting the integrity of a copyright by purchasing an authorized edition of this book and for complying with all copyright laws by not reproducing, scanning, or distributing any part in any form without permission.

ISBN 978-1-7375219-0-7
ISBN 978-1-7375219-1-4 (e-book)
Printed in the United States of America
10 9 8 7 6 5 4 3 2 1

Tattered Script Publishing: Crafting Cultural Creativity and Authenticity

Cover art and design by Lydia Manter

First Printing, 2021

For my mother, my daughters, and my granddaughters

Contents

I	Meditation Explained	1
II	The Storyteller	17
III	The Intrepid Meditator	36
IV	Jackrabbits and Snails	49
V	Why Earth?	65
VI	The Steps	94
Author's Note		121
Acknowledgments		125

I

Meditation Explained

I didn't think I would ever write a book about meditation. Aren't there enough of them out there already? Who am I to say what meditation is or how we should interpret it?

I don't think meditation should be spoken about or interpreted in language, nor should I attempt an explanation. Meditation just is. It is multi-sensory and individualistic. Maybe it is dualistic if you choose group meditation, but it is of the self. Of you. This puts me in a bit of a mess and I apologize profusely for putting thoughts on meditation into words, but how else to talk about it if not in language? Meditation can't be explained as much as I feel it is time to offer an explanation.

We're at a crossroads in our relationship to

ourselves, and unless we begin to know ourselves, truly know the self, we're going to destroy the planet and ourselves along with it. I feel this. Deeply. No matter your religion or economic status, your ethnicity or tribe, the peril we are all in is real. This isn't some apocalyptic truth. Nor do I want to scare you. We're an evolving race of people, all of us, of one planet, yet we don't know who we are. We're desperately clinging onto something, but what? It is as if the rug is being pulled out from under us on a daily basis, but we don't know what it means. The fight-or-flight response is all we have left because we're exhausted beyond measure. No one said this was going to be easy, this life, but never did we think we should be in this much distortion. Am I right?

And what is it that is distorted? Our sense of self in relationship to the one place we live — Planet Earth. It's as though we are living precariously on top of some shifting tectonic plate and rather than move with the planet, the energetic vibration, and the emotional body of our one home, we fight these shifts. We fight ourselves. We fight with each other. We fight because the planet is fighting to be. But is it possible to move with the energy of the planet? Of course it is. Is it possible to relax and enjoy life? I believe so. And is it possible to accept our place here? Who we are? Where we were born? With whom we reside? Even if it is just with ourself? Yes. Why should you trust me on this? Who am I?

My name is Alicia Cahalane Lewis. I am named after my great-grandmother Jane Cahalane Park who immigrated from Ireland in the early 1900's and my mother's college friend, Alice. I was born in Carlisle, Pennsylvania three weeks before the assassination of President John F. Kennedy. I say this because I believe it has great bearing on who I grew to be. I was never an unhappy child, but I was alarmed, I think, by life.

My parents moved to Winchester, Virginia not long after I was born. I grew up there alongside grandparents, aunts, uncles, cousins, and second cousins once removed from both my mother's and my father's side of the family. I attended John Handley High School in Winchester and graduated from Randolph-Macon Woman's College (now Randolph College) in Lynchburg, Virginia. Shortly after graduation I moved to Brunswick,

Maine where I lived for almost twenty five years with my then-husband and our two daughters.

I have now returned home to the Shenandoah Valley of Virginia to begin again, to learn to live with myself, and to discover my truth. And what exactly does this even mean? If you are reading this you were probably drawn to the book because you are curious. Perhaps you are looking for a community? A place to land? Someone or some group of people who think as you do? We're all seemingly looking for a place to land, and where that might be is where that might be. Of course we change, and our interests change, and who we are drawn to over time changes, but the one constant we all have is this: our mothers. We are all of a mother. I'm offering this book and the sixty free accompanying meditations (available on my website at *aliciacahalanelewis.com/meditations*) as a way to help bring us together because I feel it is imperative we begin to realign with our Mother Earth. This is the one thread in our woven tapestry of multi-ethnicity and gender that can ultimately help heal us.

I was born, as I said, three weeks before a seismic shift in the collective consciousness. I was born on the cusp of a cultural revolution where the past and the future had painfully begun to clash. You could say that we are all born in the midst of a seismic clash and that would be true. The planet, the people, and the cultures are always changing, adapting, pushing up against one another, and revolting. We're never a constant. So to say I was born before a historic death is merely putting me, my life, and my existence into a time frame. I was born, as all of us are born, when the planet, the people, the ideas, and always the cultures were clashing.

If we could just accept that there will never be one day that looks like the next we'd all be a lot happier because we would learn never to expect. If I expect to wake up to a sunny day and it is dreary, the sky full of dark clouds, I will be disappointed. Because I will have expected. If I wake up tomorrow expecting a raise, and it is denied, I will be angry. To wake up to a new day not expecting, but listening and finding oneself in the day rather than pushing at the day is a whole new phenomenon. I would like to tell you how it is possible and why I feel compelled to speak to this need to protect ourselves from our own self-destruction.

Growing up, acutely aware that I was longing for something, made me a wistful little girl. I was a dreamer. I wrote stories in my head and I play-acted those stories throughout my whole life, I think, to come to a place of understanding that our lives are stories. We write ourselves, and as much as this comment will be immediately disputed, bear with me as I explain. We write what we want. We might write what we expect, but for the most part we write our experiences. If, say, I am experiencing longing, as this is what I know, then I will continue to write for myself, longing. I will look at the world wistfully. I may look at a guy, an experience, a chance to publish a book, longingly, wistfully, never able to grasp it. It may continue to feel just out of reach. But as I have been trying to rewrite myself and the way I look at this self, the world around me, and the relationships I have with others, I am learning through both meditation and mindfulness that I am responsible for myself and my existence.

My mother was, at one time, responsible for me. My father too. But I am now an adult and I must care for myself. I am finding this is hard for a lot of people to accept. They expect someone to right them, to help them land on their feet, to do right by them. So they wait—and continue to wait—for help. They write a story of helplessness or expectation, but the more we add to our stories this hopelessness, or longing, or grief, the more our lives become the story and not our truth. A life lived as story can become painful. It is not a happy story. And why not? Can it not be the fairy tale? The Happily Ever After? Trust me when I tell you this: Happily Ever After isn't the end of the story. It is only the beginning of trouble because this is where the fairy tale gets real.

I grew up expecting. I grew into this story of longing, and the story continued even after I became an adult. I wrote myself to be the heroine, longing. I blame my mother who read all those moody English novels while she was pregnant with me! Somehow I absorbed the need to find my own Heathcliff and I grew up waiting for Mr. Darcy, literally and metaphysically. This is what I expected. Isn't this what we are all wishing for? Some symbolic rescue? The one thing that will help us right ourselves? Trust me when I tell you I have long since let go of thinking I need a handsome prince on a white horse to rescue me from myself. That story dissolved long ago and thank goodness for that. I have no need for a white horse unless I am going to ride it myself, but this is an example of what happens to us. We grow up expecting, and so we write/create/dream/hope what we think we are and who we should be, but nowhere are we told how destructive this practice really is. It's what we do, but I'd like to suggest we create another way.

Perhaps I'm being a bit harsh on myself, and you, by calling you out for writing a fantasy existence, but until you begin to wash away expectation you won't really understand how I arrived at this place. Believe me, this has taken me over twenty years to understand. I only wish to help you so you don't have to spend the next twenty years of your life struggling. We can transform expectation instantly through deep connections to our truth. There are many ways to get to this truth. I know people who take long walks, who putter in their gardens, who write in their journals, practice yoga, etc., and yes, these are all paths to understanding the self, because when we are quiet with ourselves we listen. This is why listening is one of the most important aspects to rewriting the script. We think we are listening to our true selves when we tell ourselves we're not good enough to publish a book, or smart enough to deserve the raise, or beautiful enough to attract love, but this is because this is the story we have told ourselves. By spending quality quiet time with ourselves, I assure you we can retrain the chattering mind to listen to the truth. We can rewrite the script.

I enjoy a long walk, puttering in my garden, practicing yoga, and looking in the mirror to gauge my sense of inner self, but these tools are simplistic and, dare I say, rudimentary. Listening to one's true self, and not the storyteller self, is difficult to do. Puttering in a garden, although enjoyable and rewarding for all the right reasons, including experiencing beauty, does not get you to the core of your truth. It will get you to an aspect of it. It will get you to happy, to rewarding, and to feeling a sense of accomplishment. It will get you to admiration for the self. These are all fine as they are aspects of what I am referring to when I say that we must find our truth, but puttering does not produce the same results as meditating. Yes, gardening is a form of meditation so please know that I understand I'm talking from two sides of the same coin here, but where I am going, and asking you to go with me through meditation, can't be achieved when our minds are on someone or something else. I cannot achieve the answers I am looking for when I am thinking about pruning roses. I just can't. Maybe you can. Maybe you will prove me wrong. But to get to the inner truth one has to be alone with oneself without activity. This is about pruning your inner rose. I will be asking you to focus on your inner self and not on anything from the exterior self. The exterior self is outside the inner self and the gardener is the exterior self, playing.

Here is another way to think about the difference between the storyteller self and the true self. The storyteller self, the writer of our own life's story, is the outside self. This is the self playacting his or her expected truth. This is the persona, the personality. This is the woman who gets up every day and wears high-heeled shoes to work because these shoes are a part of her persona, and her attitude, although by lunchtime her feet are hurting her. She refuses to change into more comfortable shoes because by changing shoes she will admit defeat. She fears that her persona will change. The heels can't win. Right? She must hail herself the champion of high-heeled shoes and wear them day after day to prove her mastery of high heels. This is her perceived truth. If you're still able to wear high-heeled shoes after spending some time getting to know your true self, I will respect you greatly as this will be your rediscovered truth, and I will understand, because I too like to wear heels. They are a part of my rediscovered truth. Should you grow to understand yourself more fully, and you decide to give away all your high-heeled shoes in exchange for something more comfortable, I will applaud you because you are finding your rediscovered true self.

The storyteller self wants to wear the high-heeled shoes. She wants to write herself as a character in heels, and so she does, day after day. The same can be said of men who wear their coats and ties and then strip them off in exchange for something more comfortable. Again, I must repeat that if you find yourself in love with your outward portrayal of yourself as authentic, whatever that may be, and you feel confident that it represents your inner self, I will applaud you. The outward appearance represents our body. It is our marker in the narrow channel of life. We all need these markers, but I am learning to respect that these markers must be true. It is time we recognize this and strip the inauthentic persona. The body, the mind, the spiritual essence, and the metaphysical self need to align to find right, to find balance. Finding balance within is an important step to take before helping to heal a tipping planet.

This meditation practice is designed to help find inner truth. It does not help to reinforce the storyteller. It is designed to help strip away the deep layers of who we think we should be for who we are. We can only do this ourself, for ourself. No one can rescue us. We must ride our own white horse, prune our own rose, and no one, not even me, should tell you how you must do this to save yourself and the planet from tipping precariously too close to more and more story and not to truth. If you feel inclined to help lessen the tilt we are creating by crafting these collective stories then I want to help you help yourself. I do not intend to tell you what to do. I want you to tell yourself what you are going to do. I am asking that you regard the notion that you're responsible, as an integral part of the planet, for her well being. By being that truthful person, you can help return the planet to equilibrium. I am asking you to become a participant, like me, in bringing ourselves and our planet back into balance.

This is my meditation series explained. The free guided/annotated meditations are available as a companion to this book, and should you ever need help understanding them you can refer back to this book as a guide. The meditations are designed to support your journey. They will simply be what they are. Words. My voice. A little background music. They are tools to help you help yourself toward your truth. Not mine. Not your mother's, your father's, or your husband's truth, but your own.

People will tell you that we learn from story. I have had many a conversation with fellow writers who adhere to this notion. They will rightly tell you that through story the human grows to exemplify its best self. I don't doubt that, but what if you take it one step farther and tell yourself that through the untangling of story you can get to know your best self? Through the ages we have moved through this understanding that we need to use stories to teach. Stories are tools. But what if you're being offered another tool such as meditation? Could you see this tool as a simpler, faster, more advanced way to get to know the true self? It's an option, one I am offering. I have repeatedly gone through multiple stories myself to reach the conclusion that by stepping away from story, or in fact stepping into it to step away from it, we can save ourselves a lot of internal/external drama down the line.

I once took on the persona of the wounded girl in need of the white knight and I lived with that story for a long, long time. So long that even when I was married and living very comfortably with two beautiful daughters and an honest, caring husband, I still felt the wretched need to look for that knight. My knight was not another man, but something I felt was missing that needed to show up in my life so that I could be rescued from my own false need to be wistful. I was longing. I didn't even know what it was I was longing for, but I was hungry, needing to throw off some character's cape and begin again with something else. And so I did. I tossed aside a perfectly adequate life for an unknown. I literally just announced to myself one day that I would take off the shell I was wearing and get real. I wanted to find me. Not my mother's version of me, my country's expectation of me, or my husband's fantasy of who I should be, but me. Just plain old uncertain me. And so I upended our lives.

I have since come to recognize the intense shedding that this required of me and the feeling that there must be a cleaner/clearer/healthier way to do this. I don't recommend upending your life. This is NOT what I am asking of you. I am simply asking you to ask yourself what is true. I am not a psychologist. I would never ask you to upend yourself, your life, or to stop therapy if that is something you prescribe to. I'm an experienced Reiki Master of Masters teacher and friend and my only agenda is to help you help yourself. Think of this book as a way to know yourself. But you must do the work. You will not lie down and be healed. You will do your own healing, and I promise you that in combination with the gardening, the journaling, the wardrobe adjustments, and the counseling, if this is what you do, you will explore deeper aspects of yourself.

Celebrity closet organizers take this approach,

but they are asking you to work on the exterior self, the self that needs purging and realigning, to get to the inner you. This little book, along with the accompanying meditations, will ask you to organize the inner self by helping you begin to throw out what no longer fits. I am offering you a way to know yourself, your Mother Earth, your relationship not only to yourself, but to the planet and all that she provides.

II

The Storyteller

Once upon a time, in a land far from here, there lived a young maiden. She was a beautiful, but wayward and sickly young girl...

If we tell ourselves we are wayward we will remain wayward. If we tell ourselves we are sickly we will remain sickly. If we adopt this story this will be our way, and if we're not careful we will reinforce this story over and over throughout every era of our existence. I made a choice to somehow throw out my story, rearrange the contents, and through meditation reintroduce myself to myself. I disassembled the wounded girl and let her grow. I won't tell you that this has always been pretty, or easy, or as successful as I might have liked, but through the unraveling, the pinching back, the rethinking, and the reimagining, I have made it to here, a place where I can look back on it all and share with you what I did to adopt more truthfulness in my life. I have gone to story to come through story to return to knowing.

You might find it interesting to note that I am striving to publish a coming-of-age novel in which a fifteen-year-old girl must go through (literally go into and through) the stories of her childhood books to heal herself from her past. She lost her mother to cancer when she was five years old and her alcoholic father left her when his wife died. This young woman, moody and lonely, has been living in a cold garret with her aunt. She is putting her focus on doing well in school, but is no longer able to play. Still grieving the loss, she finds herself on what she thinks is an imaginary island where she must rescue herself from story and return to her truth. Try selling this book idea to an agent. I can't do it. Could you? The idea for this book is so left field, or maybe it is right field, I don't know, but what I can tell you is it is not centerfield. It is not mainstream. It is not, at this time, a sellable idea. It is a progressive idea.

I want to share myself and my work as progressive. I continue to submit this book to respected agents hoping one of them will try me. Isn't this what all hopeful writers do? We go through this motion over and over. To sell ourselves, our ideas, and our visions we must first believe them ourselves. We must adhere to our own thinking, our own beliefs, our own truths. If I thought I couldn't sell this book I would have given up long ago, but I have been reworking this notion, this book, this part of myself for the better part of twenty years so that I know this young woman searching for truth. I can write her. I can take her into story, help her heal from her loss, and watch her step into her truth. By the way, I did not lose my parents this way. I am to this day very close to my mom and dad and have only made up this story to highlight my vision of self-healing. We go into and through our stories over and over throughout our lives, but they are taxing and misguiding us. To return to truth we must refrain from storytelling.

I am learning to trust the process of trying to sell myself and my ideas. It is a difficult sell, especially in a world that really doesn't trust the unknown, but this does not mean it will be impossible. Agents want books they know they can sell.

Why take on an unknown? But you know what? All writers at some point were unknowns. I find it a difficult road to travel down, continually trying to plug myself and my ideas as sound, but no one with any amount of grit gives up. Ever. It's not in our makeup. I thank the heavens I'm not a quitter, that I can trust myself and my book idea, because it was the heavens, I'm convinced, where I first went while meditating, and where I trust these ideas originated.

I no longer live in my head, in the imagined story of my life, but in the place I have made real. This is a very difficult idea to understand and subsequently communicate, but I'll give it a go. We live. We breathe. We eat and sleep and run and play. We write and read. We grow up to become mothers and fathers. Mathematicians. Astrophysicists. Survivors. Fighters. Bums. We essentially live inside a concept of a self. We can become an astrophysicist if we have the gumption to become an astrophysicist and the education to do so. We live inside concepts. We are characters in stories. For example, there is the story of the astrophysicist who went to Harvard and became a best-selling essayist and lecturer on the universe. He is this.

And I am that. And you are whatever it is you are. I am a mother, a writer, a friend. I am many more things, but I identify with these aspects of myself first and foremost. I am the sum of my parts, the accumulative chapters of my life.

The writer is an archetype, as is the mathematician, the adulterer, the bum. These archetypes are what we have made ourselves become because we have chosen to make ourselves this way, or we have chosen roads that took us to these identities. I don't believe in victimhood, nor will I blame anyone but myself for where I take myself. I can choose to blame my former husband for my unhappiness, but it is not in my makeup to do so. I am responsible for my life, the happy and the unhappy. I am responsible for how I want to be. He might have contributed to my unhappiness, because I wasn't the woman he wanted me to be and I knew I couldn't live up to that image, but he was not the root cause of my unhappiness. I am the root of my own cause and effect.

If, for example, I chose to take myself out of a marriage because I was unhappy and this landed me untethered and homeless, then I am responsible for this choice. I would have chosen this. If my former husband beat me (which mine never did, he never laid a hand on me) and I needed help to leave him, and I ignored this help, I would have only myself to blame. I, for example, might love victimhood too much to step away from this story. I might choose to stay in pain to continue this story of the victim. This makes the victim an archetype, a character in her own story. By the way, this is so terribly difficult to write about because there are too many women without the mental, emotional, or physical strength to leave their abusive husbands, and I recognize this, but if you are one to have come through this experience then I encourage you to help another. This is how I view my experiences. Have these difficulties now become the tools to help me help others?

This is difficult to explain, but I will try another approach. I personally chose to leave one story, that of an unhappy marriage, but it did not land me on the street or in a women's shelter. I have a unique situation and I am able to take care of myself without my former husband's support. This makes my situation mine. It is not yours. I have chosen not to make my former husband the enemy. I could have made him the enemy and constructed a story to hate him because I hated who I was in that marriage, but I will reiterate that I am responsible for me. He is responsible for himself. What I am responsible for I own. What he is responsible for he owns. And what we are both responsible for, our children, we both own.

I could have taken him to the cleaners because that was what was expected of me, to fight for what should have been mine, half his earnings, but I let the chips fall as I was determined they should fall. I decided to take what was mine coming into the marriage as he should take what was his. We settled all personal belongings without a fight because I didn't take what was not mine just for the sake of taking it. We were both hurting, but I'd be damned if either of us was going to become the victim. It was not in our nature. Becoming the victim would have been contributing to the story of victimhood. We both had reason to go into the role of victim, but we didn't. Instead, I went into the role of the survivor, the warrior, the nurse. I took one story and transported myself into several more, going to them to eventually come through them. And this is how I will explain storytelling.

There are multiple aspects of a person. We are

a child self, an emerging adult self, an adult, and what I will refer to as the approaching-death self. The child is the child, desperate to be cared for. A child needs. The child can learn to take care of himself/herself in time, but a child is dependent on others to care for him. This limits the child's place in the world to a role. And it puts the caregiver into a role. The child and his caregiver are in specific, what we would call necessary, roles. Sometime around ten years old the child begins to transition into an emerging adult where he is expected to do more for himself. He will make his own bed, empty the trash, clean his dishes, and put away his toys. The emerging adult (still a child) will find himself more capable of time management. If we detract from this emerging adult and stymie one fraction of what the child is capable of, the adult will not begin to emerge. He will maintain dependency. Yes, it is easier to make your ten-year-old's grilled cheese and serve it to him than it is to watch him mess up the kitchen and burn the bread, but after raising two daughters of my own and adhering to some very sage advice from my own mother, I can tell you it is far better to live with the mess then to be stuck with the hangnail of a dependent emerging adult.

Children love routine and rhythm. Thank you Dr. Wilkoff, my daughters' pediatrician, for this one. Although my girls were babies in the early 1990's, he was a stickler for early bedtime, rhythm, and routine. Maybe he was a little too Dr. Spock for my generation, but I will tell you that maintaining a schedule helped keep us all sane. We all knew what to expect. We all had a routine. There will be so many people who will disagree with this. They will argue that children need to be flexible and schedules cannot be so strict as to keep a child from adapting. I applaud you if this works for you. But ask yourself, are you running around juggling your children's lives or are you integrating all the members of your family's needs and wants? Children don't want to rule the roost. We let them, but it's unnerving for them. Integrating a schedule and child-appropriate expectations will give everyone in the household a say, a place, a voice. From experience, I believe children feel "tucked in and safe" when an adult supports them rather than coddles them. They will not act out because they feel insecure, rather they will begin to feel respected as emerging adults the more we see them as such.

The point of sharing that little aside is to help you see the roles we adopt early on in our lives. Our children adopt roles just as we adopt roles. Sometimes we repeat what our caregivers did for us with our own children, and sometimes we're not in a position to do so, or we choose not to. But a role will get created no matter how you feel about schedules or routines. I felt that to become a better parent I would acknowledge to myself, and therefore my children, that I had needs too. I wanted to teach my children early on that I too mattered. And so this approach, despite my on again/off again unhappiness with my marriage, worked very well for our little family of four. Just think how I would have struggled if I had resented my children. As they learned to take care of themselves and take on more responsibility, I began to emerge from one role and consequently took on another, that of the seeker.

My children creatively adopted their roles of child, emerging adult, and adult, and have grown into beautiful, caring women. We had more than a few bumps along the way, more than a few skinned knees, but my experience was more or less mine to have with them. I took the opportunity presented to me to create the atmosphere I understood and needed so that I could become the best mother I could be. I knew myself and I knew what I was and was not capable of. I was a capable mother within the framework of a busy day, but I was not going to become a capable mother in an unorganized chaotic day. I adapted them to me. It was my choice. I created them, in a sense, because I asked them to be organized and respectful and to look at the needs of others.

This, I will tell you, had its fair share of fits and starts, and of course I could write a whole book on raising willful teenagers, but again, the point to this aside is to share with you that I created what the role of mother, in my mind, should be. And this interpretation of mother meant that I would raise children who could sit at the dinner table throughout a meal at a very young age, clear their dishes, help with cleanup, make their beds, and pick up after themselves. They did not grow up to be waited on hand and foot. I helped them create a role that was asked of them, that of a contributor. Oh my, what a chore it was to get us all in our own unique family balance, but again, thank you, Mom, for your guidance and support!

I think we write a similar story with our spouses. We ask of them, but we ask in ways that become very constricting. Just as it may be constricting to put expectations on a child to adhere to a schedule, make their own sandwiches, use a napkin and a fork properly, and clean up after themselves, this is a form of coping by controlling their behavior. There's no fine line here, at least not one that I can see, but when we ask of a child we are, in a way, controlling the child. I needed a schedule, and I wanted my children to grow up to become self-sufficient young women, and the route I chose to do that demanded we work together. I need to put in a plug for my former husband here. We really were a good team and just knowing we had the same expectations and similar roles really helped my children find stability and continuity. A huge plus!

Now onto the spouse and that difficult transitional relationship many of us experience. How do we create a role for ourselves, and as you can see, our children, but not create a role for our spouse?

How improbable it is to leave them alone so that they can create themselves.

Often we repeat the roles we have experienced. In extreme circumstances I think some of us find ways to do the opposite of what we've experienced as children, but that takes a pretty strong, creative, self-aware person to break the cycle of a familiar role. Otherwise most of us repeat what we know. This is storytelling. This is character creating. If we create these superficial characters we will forever search for our inner truth, and we may not even realize we're searching for it, but I do believe even if we try on different clothes and hairstyles we're seeking. This can be fun and rewarding, certainly not a chore, but as much as we seek and seek and seek we're still not satisfied. The cycle repeats. We remain our own best character. We remain outside ourselves. We retain who we think we should be. We play in our own story. Fine and good, many will think. Who am I to tell you this is not a good thing? I am only here to remind you, should you be interested in understanding the level of complexity that we engage in while seeking happier, more satisfied lives, that this will take work to unpack why you might feel continually unsettled.

My experience is mine, and you'll follow other people, I'm sure, who will know from their own experiences what has worked for them. You will likely know yourself enough to know what has and has not worked for you. Maybe you got tired of changing your hairstyle years ago, but you change your mind all the time about other things. This is not a bad thing. It's an observation. Seeking truth is not settling or stopping creativity, but about accepting an inner settledness that evokes peace in yourself and ultimately, I feel, in others. If we are at peace we can help bring peace to others and to our Earth.

Crafting story is what we know, and we learn and grow through acting out scenarios. I think we can reach a level of maturity where we're not causing multiple disruptions in our own or others' lives just for the sake of acting out old outdated roles. It is through this spiritual growth where I believe we can find a place of inner acceptance. Acting gets boring, trite, unnerving. Why playact in someone else's story? Perhaps it is better to leave the stage and throw away the script. For example, I've been in several relationships since my divorce nine years ago. I probably still want a partner, although I do not want to ever marry again. I say probably because, to be honest, I still don't really know what I want. I want love. I want to feel settled. I want companionship, but marriage, no. It is hard to seek spiritual awareness (which is what I am talking about throughout this little book) through distractions. Relationships (which become my number one distraction), love, and playacting are highly addictive and rewarding for a while, because it is what we know, these comfortable old stories, but for me the outdated roles get old. Fast. I want authenticity in myself and in others. But you just can't walk up to some guy and say OK, let's throw away the script and start at authentic. That takes years of trust and a level playing field. It takes communication and awareness that we might really understand one another by understanding first ourselves.

When I got divorced I was no longer attracted to roles. I was/am attracted to love and companionship, but I no longer need nor want the role of the wife. I can do partnering better than I can do wife. Partners play on level ground. Wives, well, the very word makes me shudder. I'm not a good wife. I don't play that role well. I'm too independent, too self-reliant, and a little too into myself to ever take care of a grown adult in the role of wife. I faltered at this role. When I left the marriage I entered into other roles, other expectations, other experiences, and these too were explored, but ultimately dismissed. I make a fun girlfriend, but after a while I have found that this too needs to shift. I don't enjoy playing the role of some man's girlfriend just for the sake of playing girlfriend. Sure, I know the role, but my playing has to come from a place of authenticity, from truth, and not from being a character.

You might not visualize yourself as a character and the very idea of it might feel insulting. It is not my aim to insult you in any way. The purpose of opening up this discussion about storytelling is to help explain why my meditation series is designed the way that it is. It is designed to help you find yourself more grounded, more appreciative of yourself and therefore more at ease in your relationship to yourself and to others. Meditation is one way of accomplishing the goal of healing the past, the character, the stage. It happens to be my way so I'm here to share why this has worked for me.

Meditations aren't always designed to be easy. Sometimes they jostle you into deeper self-reflection and will require you to push through some very difficult feelings. This meditation series will help you relax, but don't expect to walk into your past and tiptoe through the tulips to heal these inner (character) wounds. Not to frighten you, but if you seek help navigating your innermost creative truth, and you want to cut through the bullshit of playing at yourself and get to real, then this is a way you could try, but you will experience wounding. By experiencing the wounding again, by revisiting it, you will heal it. Throughout this meditation series you will pull off the metaphorical band-aids you long ago slapped over those wounds, get in there and clean them out, and repair the wounds so that once they are healed they will not easily rupture and bleed again. Think of desertion as a wound, lack as a wound, trust as a wound, rejection as a wound. When these wounds are not healed but are continually patched, haphazardly, we will be forced to revisit them over and over. Real healing requires unbinding the bloody bandage and putting the wound to right. Healing these old wounds gives us a new creative voice and a greater appreciation for what we're capable of crafting.

My real is mine. It will not be yours. There will be no end of the ride in getting to real. That train car will never detach and your locomotive will always pull you forward into other aspects of yourself to explore for as long as this is something you desire. Getting to real is the journey. We will never arrive. This is difficult to tell you, but this is my truth. I am on a perpetually long ride, a forever ride, if you will, to self-discovery. This forever ride, in my experience, has been complicated and painful at times, but highly rewarding, enjoyable, fun, and playful. There will be times when I sit back and enjoy the scenery and other times when I have to get out and push this tired old locomotive up the hill. I am not exempt from difficulties but my difficulties will be mine, unique to me, as yours will be unique to you. My difficulties will be made more difficult because my mind will make them so, and you will do the same, but remember, the meaning is there if we intend for it, for healing. This is the ride we're all taking.

How we choose to go, and in what manner we choose to engage with it, or be disrupted by it, is ours. Throughout my experiences with meditation I have found that I have made unilateral discoveries about myself and my reaction to others that have helped me find a more enjoyable, peaceful ride. I'm here to help you find the same.

III

The Intrepid Meditator

As much as I am here to chat about knowing ourselves and finding the tools to do this, at the same time I will say that we are never who we think we are because we are never the same person from one moment to the next. We are constantly evolving, shifting, and rearranging pieces of ourselves. We are met with challenges, but how we pivot and shift and realize these challenges makes us unique.

How we realize and rearrange the pieces will become the most important concept that I will explain, but first I will repeat—we are engaged in story. We playact throughout our lives in situations with others to help us realize our self. We engage in scenes. We practice dialogue and even recognize when some words become more effective than others. We hone our skills at these words. We choose our reactions, the words we use, and the outcomes. Sometimes we don't know that we're choosing the outcome because emotion hinders these word choices, but by disengaging from emotion, which these meditations are designed to help do, we can rearrange and recapture truth. Through words.

I wish there was a magic wand that I could wave over these words so that we could all be healed by them, find our most effective creative self, and run through those tulips unencumbered by tragedy, or heartbreak, or death. But there are no magic wands in this work; therefore, I can't begin to create one for you.

Instead, I will offer this: The mind is our greatest enemy, our truest friend. The mind is the gateway to hopelessness or healing. The mind controls solution. It hinders outcome. It is the messy abyss or it is the beauty of our being. It is our friend and it can very much become our enemy. In short, we are what we think. What we think gives rise to what we feel. What we feel gives rise to how we react. And we can change the way we think in order to change the way we feel in order to change the way we react. Remember, there is no magic wand. Our locomotive will climb steep hills, and we can accept this knowing that we will ride this way eternally, or we can disregard it all and enjoy the hurt.

Meditation is one avenue we can take to get to know ourselves. I think of meditation as relationship with self. I know we try really hard, all of us, to reach a level of knowing by engaging in relationships with others, and we teach ourselves about ourselves through these relationships, but ultimately it is the relationship with self that needs to heal so that we can find our whole. We can't continue to search through the lens of others. It's just no longer possible. Think of Facebook as the ultimate teaching tool to help us return to our self. Mind you, it will appear backwards, as many teaching tools often do. It is as though some giant disrupter, whose name just happens to be Mark Zuckerberg, tossed out from his bag of tricks this destructive way for us to look outside ourselves, and to look for approval from others in ways that will never satisfy us, to help teach us about ourselves. By engaging in the words and the actions of others without thinking, but by reacting, we create these disjointed aspects to the self. This is not how we become authentic.

Social media is simply a tool to teach us, through disruption, one of the stories we perpetually like to stay engaged in by introducing us to what we might not want. I did say it was backwards, but when we can look through the lens and see both sides we will begin to see all the teachers we are going to meet in this lifetime. It just so happens that Mark Zuckerberg is, from my understanding, a disrupter, a teacher, a guide. And how did I come to understand this? Through meditation. He is here to show us how destructive we can become should we choose this path of putting ourselves outside the vision of our true selves.

As seductive as social media is, it is a story that is designed to take us away from ourselves to lead us back toward ourselves. Bear with me as I explain. By using a tool such as social media and all its angling, posturing, and persuading (great aspects of a story), it becomes impossible for us to see the true self because it is impossible to see a true self through the lens of others, through this much disruption. The only way to find the self, approve of the self, love the self, trust the self, and become your true self is to go to self and get to know yourself as yourself. Then you can share yourself. I think of Facebook as the ultimate tool to help us know precisely what it is we want to recognize about storytelling. It is the destroyer of self. It brings us to lack, to the hole, to the abyss, because it takes us to want and the need for more and more approval and recognition. It takes us to bigger chasms. To more internal angst.

We are collectively seduced by holes and by lack. We are drawn to lack like ants to sugar. Mark Zuckerberg is tempting us with this bait. Will we ever be able to recognize how we're seduced by lack and ultimately regain our footing? This is an old story, one we play in over and over. Falter and find. Redemption and rebirth. I, for one, don't feel the need to play in Mark Zuckerberg's polarity story. Yes, I have these social media accounts, and yes, I do use them, but I do see them for what they are and I have hired someone to post for me. This is my way of staying out of the seductive sugar. Is it necessary that I post? Probably not. Do I want to share my work? Yes. Is it the best way to share it? It is at this time. So I engage without really engaging and I encourage you, should you ever feel disenfranchised by social media, to limit your engagement with it. It will take you to empty calories, but not to substance.

These are harsh words for social media, but I stand by them. I stand by them because over and over I have received guidance through meditation that helps me discern that this is my truth. Is this going to become your truth? I don't know. I will leave that up to you. You are your own intrepid meditator, adventurer, pioneer, scout. You are your own body, your own mind, your own finger-pointing, tail-wagging bundle of joy or sadness. Should you desire something more for yourself, but you can't get out of your way to find a solution, may I suggest meditation? It is a tool. You will have to use it to dig with. You will need to work. But if this interests you, and you would like a traveling companion of sorts, this is what I am offering.

I am offering Reiki-inspired healing through meditative language to help you take some of your own self-healing steps. Take a moment to pause, to feel, to rationalize this information. Does this resonate with you? I have a Masters in Creative

Writing and I am a master level Reiki healer and teacher. Does this matter? It will to some. I have credentials. To others, these are just fluffy words that will have no bearing on what it feels like to read them. Words are seductive, much like an advertisement, and I know I'm attempting to pull you in to read these words, but at the same time, honestly, I won't feel what you feel about them, how they make you respond, if they bring you joy, disappointment, frustration, or uncertainty. Meditation can be unsettling and either we walk through this uncertainty knowing that this kind of uncertainty exists, or we get pulled further and further away from our true selves because we fear what we are going to discover.

Reiki is a solution if you see it as such. It is a possibility, a respected approach to energetic healing. It is a name brand, recognizable. It is a label. It is a vocabulary word to define a particular form of energetic movement in the body, the home, the atmosphere. I think of Reiki as a term used to describe healing. Period. It has a respected place in our lexicon because through time, experience, and multiple practitioners and teachers, it has proven effective. It will work if you believe it is working.

I have to be very careful as I say this, and I will say it again. Reiki works because the mind trusts. Your mind is as much a part of the healing process as is the practitioner, and if you don't have a fluid mind a practitioner can only do so much for you. You are responsible for you. A Reiki practitioner is fortified by your trust in the work. If your mind doesn't trust you won't receive the healing, and/or you will hurt more as a result. You will dismiss Reiki. You will forever dismiss a possibility. The mind, the most important aspect of healing the self, will only find disillusionment, or fear, or resign itself to hurt, and as a result you will maintain/sustain this level of hurt. Your mind will control you.

Reiki is a tool. These words are tools. These words in combination with some of the Reiki intention behind them will either bring you fulfillment or they will dissuade you. We live in a polarity of emotion and motion. We live in an ever-increasing push/pull of right or wrong, this or that, hot or cold. I do believe that this cold will get colder, that the right will get righter, the wrong wronger, and the black blacker. Why? As Earth's magnetic energy continues to shift we will shift too. As magnetic north shifts, which happens on the planet periodically, we will get more and more emotionally pulled to hold our ground. The right will need to be right. The left will need to be left. The weight will need to be measured.

Scientists who study the phenomenon of Earth's tilt do not measure emotion. They measure rising sea levels which are contributing to this tilt, because as Earth heats up and the ice melts, oceans rise. As the melting seawater redistributes itself, the weight of this redistributed water causes Earth's axis to shift. I just happened to hear this on The Weather Channel while I was writing this section of the book. Earth's poles have shifted thirteen feet since 1980. This reported theory supports the guidance that I have received in my own meditations, but scientists do not study how this shift affects our inner balance. As Earth moves we move. Perhaps it is time to study how we are physically and emotionally altered by this shift. I am not a scientist. I do not study climate change. My information has come to me through other channels. By listening, I have received guidance about our connection to the planet and the way our minds tilt in relationship to the planet's tilt.

Our minds, in search of balancing, or centering, will crave solution, but the more we crave centering, the more the need to become one way or the other will become a disservice. We will need an honest centering, but my center is not yours. And vice versa. If we're not careful our polarity will become more and more extreme as many of us make this gigantic push to be right. But remember, there is no right. Right is in the mind of the beholder. Through this meditation series you will be asked to go to balance. To centering. There is no right. There is only your truth in relationship to my truth. In balance.

The meditations that accompany this little book are designed to help curb this insatiable desire to need a right. They are a tool to help balance the polarity, the pull to the hard right or hard left. (I realize that this sounds like I'm making a political statement by using these two vocabulary words, but this is not about politics; it is about extremism which is being playacted out in the political arena.) The meditations are only as sustainable as you are sustained by the notion of them, and they will not work for you unless you work in conjunction with them. They are not a magic wand. They are not designed to take you down a lazy river on an inflatable raft ever marveling at the beauty and ease of your trip. These meditations are coal-mining meditations for the coal miner in you. You will excavate. You will marvel at yourself when you discover and then release an important block in your psyche, but these meditations will not take you to Reiki so that you can get "healed" by them. They are designed to help you rediscover your own inner healer by using my words as tools. If we can think of ourselves as destroyers we most certainly can begin to think of ourselves as healers. We can be both. We are both. And we must balance the part of us that wants to hurt with the part of us that craves healing. I won't be your most beneficial teacher, friend, traveling companion if I do the excavating for you. You will do it for yourself, but I am here to help.

Reiki purists might complain about what I am doing in offering these words to you, and so to explain further I will offer the following statement: Reiki is a form of healing long guarded and protected as sacred. I honor this. It is reserved for those willing to study and use this tool with compassion, respect, and an understanding that it is sacred. I honor this. Reiki is a tradition. I honor this. It is a spiritual transponder of sorts designed to take you to yourself through your own spiritual gateway. Reiki heals the body, the mind, the spirit. I honor this. My intention is to honor Reiki not by divulging the sacredness of it, but to use my relationship to Reiki, which is mine, translate this healing work into vocabulary words, and put words to the work. The words are infused with sounds which help transport emotion. By transporting and lifting emotion from the body we can heal the body of hurt. Reiki is the vocabulary word I am using to describe my intention. The words are imbedded with the codes. The words are my way of sharing what I have been guided to share. We are all capable of finding our inner truth and we all deserve a gateway to help us reach out highest creative potential.

The meditations are constructed simply to put language to intention. They are not some big Reiki reveal. I respect the sacredness of the Reiki community so I will not share what is not mine to share, but it is important I explain why I am using the terminology that I am. Language is sacred. All language, to those who treasure thinking, is sacred and special. Therefore, Reiki is a way to transport intention, and only by transporting intention can we begin to find truth.

IV

Jackrabbits and Snails

I am a snail. I make slow deliberate moves. I am not quick to shift, but when I do, I do so easily and confidently. I want to take one recognizable road to help me become a stronger, more aligned individual. I don't want to skip about trying on different personas or approaches to reach my intended goal of Divine Awareness. I have been at times jackrabbit-like, but only to move myself along when I was stuck. I have taken unpredictable leaps of faith on this road to awareness, and it has all been good, and for the most part, comfortable, but I prefer being this metaphorical snail over being the rabbit. I like to see what is up ahead and I want to study it awhile before arriving.

A metaphorical snail favors insight over speed.

A jackrabbit favors speed over insight and will usually have to go back and forth a few times to garner all the pieces of themselves they are trying to capture, to contain, and thereby embody. This is not a problem, merely an observation. One is not better than the other. One is one and the other, the other. You will get to where you want to be, if you choose this journey of looking within, no matter the speed. We call this Divine Awareness. Within this framework there is no time. It just is.

You are Divine Awareness. You are your own creator, making you divine, making you aware of yourself not only as a creative, but as the spiritual essence of creator. We are creatives creating. Naturally, we think of artists as creators, but mathematicians, scientists, coal miners, and estheticians, to randomly name a few, are all creators. We all create life for ourselves. Breath is life, and because we all breathe, we all create. The idea of a creator is such a difficult concept to apply to ourselves. Why? The idea that we are Divine Creators is absurd, right? How can we, having fallen from Grace, be the creator figure? Well, we have to think of ourselves as living, breathing beings, and once we acknowledge that we live and breathe we will see that in order to go on living we have to create breath. By creating breath we create life.

It's difficult to use terms like creator or god or supreme or divine on ourselves. We want to look outside ourselves for those beings, and so we will, but to look within and find divinity we need to apply the concept of godliness to ourselves. If God is a vocabulary word meaning to give life, to support life, to sustain life, to repair life, to heal life, and to transport us to death how then can we find balance within us that puts some, if not all, of these same responsibilities back on ourselves? Again, this is for you to answer. We look outside ourselves, but are we looking within? Once we are able to look within I think we will be able to look at ourselves as divine. Giving life. Supporting life. Repairing life. Healing life. Transporting ourselves to death.

Might I suggest a name for this? I will admit using the term god or creator when thinking about myself is difficult. It's doable, but difficult. It's a stretch of the imagination that borders on perverse. You will either get me on this one or you won't, and that's OK. I'm not saying I'm God. I'm saying that I am divine. No one is my master. I am my own master. How then can I believe in God and not recognize Him as master? I recognize God as within me. He is not ruling me or standing watch. He is not telling me what to do or who to be. I am giving myself to God to become god. This is an old paradigm that will either resonate or not. God, to me, is me because I am from All. I am a fraction of All, and I recognize that I am a fraction, but a fraction is still part of the whole.

I see myself as a fraction. I see myself as a giver and protector of life. I give myself life through breath and I protect myself in life by continuing to breathe to continue life. Remember, we tell ourselves stories and myths. We teach dogma through story. We teach through parable. We teach by telling ourselves truths that have been passed down by generations of others. Sometimes truths change. Truth becomes subjective, and time, irrelevant. Truth is what we believe it to be at any given moment. It is our truth now. I know that I am me. I hold life. I see myself as life. I don't need to live in a past story that crowns the title, Bearer of Life, to one person, one goddess, one martyr, one God. No. It is 2021 and I am aware that I am a living, breathing creator thereby giving me access to my own divinity. Divinity is not reserved for a select few. It is for us all.

Is this a story? It could be, but it is a story that has come around again. I believe we have been living on the cusp of a change for a long time now and we are witnessing an uprising of sorts, especially in countries where we might have more personal freedoms, to explore this notion of divinity. In the United States there is a clash of thinking going on right now and the upheavals we are experiencing arise from this polarity of thinking. Is God to be altered to our own version/ideal and can we do this within Christian churches? Of course we can. Our image of God has and will continue to change through time. God is as malleable and diverse as we are. God isn't just one thought. Our version of God is always shifting. I, for one, don't prescribe to religious doctrines, but that doesn't mean that I'm not a spiritual person. I could worship a triangle and believe it to be the Holy Trinity. Who knows, maybe math and religion will one day find themselves in conversation? My point being that math can be religious in nature if we see it as such, but we don't. We see math as absolute and religion as subjective. I think we should have more tolerance for God as a geometric figure, but that is another book altogether, one that might get written by someone other than me! The triangle is a conceptual image, one we can identify with. God is not. God is then made into someone who can become conceptualized. We create images representative of who we are within our respective cultures. God then begins to fit an image. We are who we are because we create ourselves. God is who God is because of how we craft image.

Cultural ideals change quickly during periods of intense unrest and more slowly during times of peace. When there is a lot of cultural unrest it can begin to feel really unsettling and we will feel like we just want to put the genie back in the bottle and make it all "right" again, but once that genie has been unleashed it's pretty hard to put him/her back. Therefore, I believe in empowering the self. I believe in honoring the innate ability within us all to care for the self which will give us more control over our own lives. We should not be dictated to, forced, or coerced. We should be given the freedom to grow and shape ourselves as we see fit, but, in truth, we will always be a part of something larger, more powerful, more deceptive, more controlling. We will always is a very strong statement. Perhaps I should say I will always, in my lifetime, be part of a central government that controls the division of tax money I pay to it each year. I am a part of a revolving wheel. I know this and I live with the knowledge that I can contribute to the direction this wheel will turn by voting, but whether I like it or not this wheel will turn. This is our story. This is what has been created.

Creations shift all the time, and when we are a part of a shift, as every generation will be, there is fear. We clash. Tensions arise when no one understands the cultural shift or can control the outcome. But things will always shift and change. Things will appear terrible and deathly until they appear more peaceful. We create these wars. We are responsible for the flux.

Earth is the constant creator always changing. She literally moves mountains. Through my meditations I have been helped to stay balanced in all this movement. This is why I take you down into the heart of Earth through meditation to connect to Earth so that you will stay grounded and move with Earth to shift yourself. If we stay outside of the Earth experience, perhaps above it and not connected to it, our earthly experiences will float out into the ether. To be of Earth we must balance our Earth self with this more heavenly ideal. I am trying my best to understand that by being of the Earth we can transform. As I am learning and growing and ascending I am also learning to teach.

Earth is the metaphorical jackrabbit as she is the snail. She can literally change her course instantly as with a volcanic eruption or earthquake (the jackrabbit), or move incrementally season after season into different climate sequences (the snail). These snail movements are slow until they are not. Suddenly, her patterns of shift becomes apparent and we become alarmed by this sudden change of events, but the climate is always changing and will continue to shift incrementally. When we notice the shift will be when we notice it. For the short amount of time that we have been studying climate and Earth temperatures, we have a pretty good idea of where Earth was and how she has changed, but because we can't predict where she is going we have this fairly good-sized alarm bell ringing right now, and rightfully so, that we need to slow down the heating and bring the planet back into balance.

Earth is a living, growing, moving, shifting polarity. She is never a constant. Earth moves every day in some way. She moves around the sun thus making motions such as seasons. These seasons are fairly consistent, but there will be times when she gets out of balance. This will cause oceans to dry up or ice to melt. This happens whether we drive cars or not, but we are accelerating these climate changes by driving cars and emitting more carbon dioxide than we are creating oxygen. The planet is out of balance.

We are meant to be stewards of the planet. To be a responsible steward of the planet I must choose not to harm her. This is very, very difficult to do in a modern world. I can choose not to buy or consume food in plastics, for example, and as much as I try to do this, I need to do better. I can choose not to drive a gas-guzzling car, but where I live the car-charging options are limited. I could and probably should petition for electric charging stations, and if I did that I might see my community embrace this change, but I don't live in the most environmentally woke municipality. I need to be patient, as this change will likely come to this area, but I think there is a lot of concern about the amount of energy it takes to produce a battery. To many, battery production is equally as harmful as emissions. I could ride my bicycle but there are a lot of hills and a lot of miles between my house and the store. I could choose to live where I could walk, but where I live all the grocery stores, as one example, have left the neighborhoods. I can't change this overnight, but what I can do is limit the number of times I get in the car to go to the store. I never go for one or two items. I consolidate errands and do them all on one day. I limit the number of times I take my car out. These are small steps, but ones I have decided to take.

Earth *will* shift. I can't stop Earth from shifting violently when there is a volcanic eruption, a forest fire, or an earthquake, but by recognizing this relationship with her I begin to acknowledge Earth as my home. Why would I ever want to chip away at the foundation of my home and destabilize it? I don't. I choose to care for the planet in the small ways that I can. I tend a garden and grow some of my own vegetables. I do not add chemicals to my lawn. My grass is not as lush as my neighbor's grass, but I am fine with that. (In all honesty, I should just remove the water-dependent grass entirely and put in native plants.) These efforts are not nearly enough, but they are steps, ones I feel we should all begin to take. The accompanying meditations are designed to help you align with Earth in ways that will help you recognize your relationship to her. These meditations are not absolutes. They are subjective and open to interpretation. I am merely here to get you started.

We will have many teachers in our lives. I feel really fortunate to have met many who have helped me attain balance by teaching me the skill of deep and mindful meditation. Once I was taught some of these key foundational elements, I could then take them and expand them to fit my particular energy pattern. My energy pattern is mine. It is not yours. Remember, we're fractions, part of the whole. I will acknowledge that this meditation technique will work for some, but not for all. It has been designed to appeal to the beginner and the more advanced meditator, but all of us are beginners to some extent, when we come to a new class and are taught by a new teacher. By expanding our awareness, and trying something new, we begin to open up avenues that will take us to other parts of ourselves. Maybe your way of meditating has worked for you for years, and you're thinking, no, these vocabulary words aren't mine. I invite you to try substituting language that works for you for my language. By using our own vocabulary words we can expand our awareness into others' ideologies and see that we are all ruminating on very similar, if not identical, ideas. Vocabulary causes us to clash, but these meditations are never intended to upset or insult, rather to inform and instruct.

To become an intrepid meditator, a self-studying pioneer, avatar, captain of our own ship who is fearless, loves exploration, and welcomes innovation, we don't need to identify whether or not we're the metaphorical jackrabbit or snail. We are probably both. We can take things on the fly as much as we might study, ruminate, and take our time. There will be various areas of interest where we feel we're a quick study and other areas where we will need time to think through a decision. I don't like being a jackrabbit, but I must admit there are times when I do react like a rabbit, quick to jump in, quick to bounce around, quick to "hop to it," and this has worked for me. When I must slow things down to be patient and take my time moving in my mind, as well as in my body, from one idea or one location to another, I can lose patience with this at the same time I am here to say this has been beneficial. Slowing down to ruminate has given me added awareness that I can be specific in my thinking. This doesn't mean I can't or won't change my mind, but it does mean I have grown to know myself so that when I do make a quick decision it is a truthful decision based on introspection. By slowing down, studying, and meditating, my actions then become deliberate. Rather than appear like I'm bouncing around, the decisions are actually well studied and acted upon without guilt or indecision. I jump in because I know that they are truthful decisions. By balancing the jackrabbit with the snail I become the best of both approaches. The snail approach helps me become a more patient person and the jackrabbit approach gives me the impetus to take deliberate actions.

I am simplifying this radically. I am pushing a theory of thinking into a very small parameter. We are never either/or, but both. We are not just a mother/father, but a mother/father and a woman/man with our own needs and desires. We're not just a woman/man with our own needs and desires, but a mother/father with additional responsibilities for taking care of another. Being a jackrabbit and a snail is about being responsible for ourselves, and if we're a mother or a father we will recognize that we are responsible for another. Being a jackrabbit might push us to be quick-tempered, but by embracing the snail we can slow down and think before reacting. Balancing ourselves will radically help balance our relationships with others as this will help us attune not only to ourselves but to the ways and feelings of our loved ones. When we are in balance with ourselves, and our relationships, we can begin to attune to our relationship with the planet. Being in balance, as part of the planet, we can turn what we are (balance) toward another (Earth) and help heal this tipping ecosystem we're living in.

When we are out of balance, and the planet responds to this, we create more imbalance not only within ourselves, but on the planet. In my meditations I am repeatedly shown just how responsible I am not only for myself, but for Earth. I am responsible, energetically, for the health and well-being of myself, my offspring, and the home I inhabit. I take this responsibility very seriously. I am of the planet and therefore a part of the planet, and I have been working toward understanding that this makes me, Alicia, the planet.

Here is another way to think about this. I am a part of, a fraction of Earth. I am a part of the whole. Being a part also makes me of the whole. I am beginning to see myself of the whole which makes me the whole itself. Earth. That one may take awhile to digest, but it's worth accepting that the fraction is of the whole making us all part of one body, one planet, one ecosystem. We are (our bodies) the ecosystem because we are of it.

I grew up with a very deep understanding of the responsibility we have to one another. This was my family's and my community's modus operandi. I lived and continue to live in that same community where caring for others is paramount. Time and sentiments have changed radically since I was a young girl, but our communities, and the planet itself, are still fragile ecosystems that need our help. We can't ignore ourselves, our families, our neighbors, or the planet. We're doing this and we're all suffering. Being a jackrabbit is about jumping in to know yourself, to trust yourself, and understand who you are in this gigantic puzzle called life. It's also important to slow down like the snail and study the pieces of yourself, discard what does not fit, and begin to push the puzzle pieces around until you find the right alignment not only for yourself, but within your relationships.

These meditations are designed to teach you about relationship, the awareness that we are in contrast to or in accord with. By consolidating the guided information and simplifying it (I think you'll be really grateful I've kept it simple), these meditations will look and feel accessible. That's the idea behind this whole approach. We are of this planet. We are not separate from her. It is my greatest wish to simplify your life by offering you a way to look at yourself that teaches you not only how easy and painless a life can become, but to share with you my personal journey as a way to help you understand the importance of taking time out of your busy (are you really that busy or just distracted?) life.

V

Why Earth?

I have to ask the question, why Earth? Why offer a meditation series now? Why associate meditation and Earth in the same sentence? Can meditations originate from Earth? The answer to this is yes. My meditation series takes you down into the heart of Mother Earth to help you ground to the planetary energy of the Earth while lifting you from the stagnant energies you've been holding in your body to a higher plane of awareness. These meditations are designed to use Earth as your healing modality.

We often think of meditation as something that will take us off of the planet and into a higher state of being, and that was an original stepping stone to help us expand awareness, but these meditations are designed to return us to our core, the planet, in ways that bring the expansive energies into the body where we can hold onto them and use these expanded energies more successfully. Think of your experience as part of a circle of continuum.

This meditation series is designed to take you further into this idea of exploration and expansion. We're Earth bodies playing in some very difficult energies that keep us stuck in old patterns. Because Earth has consistent patterns, ones of growth and destruction, light and dark, right and left, up and down, we're trapped in these polarities of our own making. Earth has swallowed us hook line and sinker into these patterns, but does this have to be the only way we live? Trapped in a continuum of birth, death, and rebirth? Maybe? This might be your story. Increasingly, I've been working on a new pattern for myself where I ride this wave of creativity rather than being toppled by it. By being of the Earth, rather than part of Earth, or outside of Earth, I am finding balance. Rather than think of myself as on the planet, I am beginning to think of myself as of the planet, as the planet itself. If, in a meditation, I can enter the Earth's core then I can attract the original star blueprint of the planet for my own well-being. After all, if we're attracted to the heavens why can't the heavens be right here where the original star codes exist? Inside the planet? Cannot the planet become your own heaven?

Rather than think of the planet as something magnificent and otherworldly and therefore divine, we go outside of the difficult experience of our Earth lives to search for someplace better. This is an old story, one I feel should be rewritten. Earth is of the universe. Isn't that what we think of as our heaven? Out there? Well, isn't Earth out there too? It is. Earth is as much out there as any other example of someplace in space.

I would like to invite you to stop thinking about heaven as there and Earth as here. It's perhaps a new thought, or one you've already had for years, but together we could think about Earth as heaven, a place in the universe that came from starlight, and is nothing but stardust with an enormous advanced ecosystem. Could you begin to see yourself as much nowhere as you are everywhere? Earth is nowhere as it is here. We've marked heaven as out there by our own design.

By returning to the planet and focusing first and foremost on the core of the planet's energy, I hope to encourage you to find your grounded center in your Earth body. Your cellular body is of Earth, and by going through DNA to reach the outer bands of consciousness we can begin to return to the planet's original DNA. By returning to the original blueprint we can return to ourselves and the heart of what it means to live here. Yes, we're encouraged to live in harmony with the planet, but this is increasingly difficult to do. We're opposed to new thinking. We're in opposition, not only to our own ideas, but to the ideas of others. There's nowhere to go where we can get a "right" answer. One person's right is another person's wrong. It has always been this way, and for the foreseeable future this is the way it will continue, but this doesn't mean we have to fight about it. We can live in balance with all the ideas.

I invite you to engage with a more meditative self to expand your awareness of a more balanced self. By doing so we can begin to heal the planet from all the heartbreak we seem to throw onto her. Yes, I know Earth throws it back at us, but that is because we're not in balance with Earth.

She throws back what we give her and we, in turn, fight ourselves, as well as the planet, for survival. What if, and this is as ancient as the oldest civilizations, we tried to live in harmony with the planet, encouraged a more balanced relationship with her, and didn't live to fight with her, but to share her? My kumbaya moment. Right? Well, believe it or not that's what these meditations are designed to do—give you back your harmony.

I'm going to be really straightforward about something I will admit might be a difficult pill for some of you to swallow. The planet is way out of balance. Maybe you can see this. There are some places on the planet where it is easier to live than other places, and yet we continue to try to carve out a life on coastal tidal lands and in arid deserts. We do this by choice and by necessity. There are many of us who have and many more who do not. We're asked to share, and many of us do share a portion of our good fortune with others, but there are many of us who do not.

My advantages in this lifetime have afforded me an opportunity to spend long (and when I say long I do mean long) hours studying these healing modalities. I have "worked" at this job for two decades. During this time I did not hold a full-time job. I was a stay-at-home mom and the recipient of a generous family. My struggles were not monetary, but emotional. True, monetary struggles bring on emotional struggles, but by being free of monetary difficulty I was afforded the time to work on these meditations, and this is why they are free of charge. I plan to donate this little book to many. I was gifted an Earth experience that brought me financial stability and in turn I'd like to offer a gift of emotional stability in kind.

I've experienced some very difficult personal relationships that were heartbreaking, including a twenty-two year marriage and a divorce. Yet they did not leave me scared to love myself, to love life, or to love others. I am actually able to acknowledge the beauty and the benefit of these relationships as personal growth experiences. The laundry list of these experiences is long, but, in a nutshell, I have struggled to sustain partners. I love men. Love them madly and dearly. I love them, and I know that I am loved by them. But men, well, they seem to need a woman to need them. I don't need men. I love men. I love their quirks and their difficulties, but I don't need to prop them up. I don't need propping up. I feel more comfortable in friendships where men don't need me to be anything other than my true self. And who knows, maybe one day that will shift?

The heartbreak these relationships have caused me has been substantial. I have put on a happy face over the years, but truly my heart was often breaking. I just couldn't connect to the traditional roles expected of me. If I could have waved a magic wand (there I go again!) over each of my romantic relationships, I would have wished for better balance. I would have wished for the antiquated roles that we played in to vanish. In my perfect world men would be able to prop themselves up without me propping up their egos, and I, well, I wouldn't try so hard to nurse them out of some wounded place. In turn they wouldn't be intimidated by me, or talk for me, or put me into their own version of what they want, but don't have, in a woman.

These meditations have given me insight into this complicated relationship we have with need. Need is a complex emotion that traps us into thinking we are incomplete. We don't need to sustain fantasies of ourselves. We can be whole without partnering. We can be whole without want. I may desire a partner, but I am in the very fortunate position not to need a partner, and yet emotional need has trapped and entangled me into feeling such loss. These meditations have helped me discern. Need is a fault line. Should we all come through this tidal wave of emotional complication maybe there will be opportunities where we share who we are in more truthful ways rather than need to prove we are someone we're not. An inability to acknowledge/accept our true self ultimately leads to heartbreak and expectation.

Earth is a tidal wave of distrust. I feel strongly that this is because we distrust ourselves as ourselves. We distrust who we are so in this quest to figure it all out we throw in the towel toward others. Life is so easily tangled. I have contributed to the distrust because I didn't know who I was supposed to be any more than the rest of us. But by dissecting myself, picking out what no longer fit, rearranging the pieces, and making room for more of my true self to find its way to me, I am beginning to understand just how important, helpful, and healing this process can become. Think of yourself as a landscape puzzle. All the pieces from multiple puzzles have been thrown, alongside yours, down onto a table. Your puzzle pieces are mixed in with your mother's, your father's, your community's, your school's, your lover's, your daughter's, etc. pieces. The list is endless. We absorb and surround ourselves with multiple pieces of multiple puzzles.

My puzzle will have a different shape and landscape design than yours, but I might be your best friend as you are mine. Certainly, I will want some of your puzzle pieces to fit because I resonate with them, or you, and I will want us to get along. Therefore, I might begin to wear the same clothes you wear, cut my hair like yours, and shop for the same end tables. You get the idea. I will know myself through you. But what happens when these pieces of your self and my self begin to tangle? Suddenly, I don't know where I might begin and end. I might have acquired some pretty fantastic end tables through it all, but are they truly mine? The only way I'm going to know if my new end tables, which match yours, are truly mine is to remove my emotional attachment to your puzzle and begin to look more closely at my own. It might be that the end tables are perfect. They fit the style of my room. I belong with those tables as much as the tables belong with me. But what happens when I discover that the tables were perfect for you, but not for me? Does this mean we can't be best friends? Of course not. It means you should decorate to your liking, and I, well, I'm going to have to explore other options.

I wish I had known this when I was married. I mean of course I knew it, intellectually, but I was tangled and in distress. I wasn't old enough or experienced enough to recognize just how badly my former husband wanted me to become a part of his puzzle. He didn't know he was doing this, and at the time I didn't recognize the game. God bless him. Truly, I love him still, but I was young and uncertain too. He wanted all of my pieces to fit into his landscape design, but I didn't know how to be my own individual alongside another. As I matured, and grew to understand that our two puzzles were very, very different, I was so tangled I couldn't even begin to recognize the pieces of myself, let alone him. So I threw in the towel. I needed to begin again, take my puzzle pieces away, resist the temptation to let someone else design me, and work this out by myself. In hindsight, I learned you don't have to throw in the towel and start over, but I was so distressed and drowning. (This distress, by the way, was not his fault. He was trying to help me, or so he thought, but at the end of the day it wasn't helpful to take my puzzle pieces for himself and put them into his end game.) Although we were both in this pattern together, we were never able to articulate it to work our way out of it.

I have heard his current girlfriend (think Modern Family—we're still close and socialize together on occasion) remind him not to "lobby." When I heard her say this the first time I had such an aha moment. She nailed it. He is so good at lobbying and advocating for his own vision/version of how to be alive in this world, that he continues to run you aground trying to get you on board, but this, I now know, is because he is terribly anxious to find his own footing so he is going to be damn well certain you find it for him too. I have to remind myself and our daughters that it's on us to recognize this.

Earth has magnetic pull. We have magnetic, emotional pull. Earth, if we could go into the very heart of her, and we do in these meditations, speaks. She is a presence, a life source/force of her own. We advocate for ourselves, but we're less inclined, all of us, to advocate for Earth. There are some of us far more tuned into the planet than others, but we're all jumbled pieces of this life force. Who are we in relationship to her? If we tell ourselves the story of sin, and we look at sin as a marker, we will live up against and experience sin. We will write this as the relationship we have to the planet. We will see sin in ourselves and others. If we write the story of heartbreak we will live and experience a breaking heart.

I'm growing to understand that Earth didn't give me heartbreak. God didn't give me heartbreak. I drew heartbreak into my landscape puzzle. It's what I thought belonged. Wrong! So how did I get out of this jumble? Through much wrangling and meditation I removed the puzzle piece marked broken heart from my heart and from my mind. I had played with that piece long enough. I removed this piece, belonging in an old story, or maybe someone else's story, from the pile. I was trying to fit it in, but it wasn't quite fitting. You know when you think you have the right piece, it's so close in shape and size to the open space where you need one to fit that you force it to work, only to discover that this is not the right piece after all? That it came out of a different box? That's what I discovered about myself. I was trying to fit an old emblematic structure into a modern design.

Why, you ask, didn't I see this, and why would I go through experience after experience until I figured out this outdated emotional pattern? Bottom line, Earth is difficult to navigate. She wraps us up in her embrace then spits us out to glean what she has to offer. We're literally and figuratively on our own. But help, we cry! The last thing we want is to be on our own. Don't we deserve a helping hand? Unconditional love? That's many a story, but the more we need a hand the less we help ourselves, and the less we help ourselves the more we feel alone as we continue to look for help outside ourselves. The circles continue, over and over. I was looking for help, someone to put the broken heart piece somewhere. Anywhere. I couldn't grasp that love wasn't about being broken. That it was about longing. This is what I came into this world feeling, that love hurts. Remember, I drank from the breast of a mother grieving the loss of a president. I do believe that somehow I drank the grief of a nation. Maybe I had to experience a broken heart so I could write about it and share this healing modality with you. Who knows? But this is what I've chosen to do.

By navigating emotional Earth we navigate physical Earth. Emotional Earth and physical Earth are lovers. They are entwined. Emotional Earth says hurt. Physical Earth says hurt. Emotional Earth is always in distress thus making physical Earth very much in distress too. We're the emotional/physical byproducts of this love affair. Well, let's be honest. Earth didn't say hurt. Earth said, "Here's a bit of shade and some water. Now have a go of it and try not to kill yourselves over it all." We aren't listening to Earth. She's our home, our mother, but she gives us what we make of her. If we see sin she gives us sin. If we see heartbreak she gives us heartbreak. We follow people who hurt us. We're entrapped in governments that destroy our liberties. We're lemmings. We're dignitaries. We're contraction as we are expansion. We're helpless. We're helping. In one lifetime we could live many different lives of struggle and hope, of loss and gain. This is our world. We are where we are at any given moment and what we experience becomes the way we view Earth.

I don't know why so many souls hurt as much as they do and bring hurt upon themselves and others. It boggles the mind. This meditation series can't answer that question. These souls don't want to heal. They want to hurt. Earth is a polarity. We will have two sides of the same coin until we don't. If the idea of helping rather than hurting Earth would help you gain insight into your own creative self, then these meditations are for you. We can't change minds overnight. We can only change our own. As creative as we are, we are equally destructive. We create and destroy only to recreate the creation again and again. Ideas need to shift, and as we grow and learn hopefully we will all take better care of ourselves, one another, and the planet. Until that day arrives when we can all see the ridiculousness of this reoccurring mindset of hurt and healing, we will live and die and rebirth ourselves repeatedly. This can happen in one lifetime. It will happen in multiple lifetimes, and if we can trust the archangels who will work with us in these meditations, we will grow to respect the difficulty of trying multiple lifetimes as a struggling peasant or as a toad. Honestly, I don't know the full story. I do have an understanding from participating in meditation that we are living to be reborn and that we are continually, yet falsely, creating an Earth story.

We're a fraction of Earth's life cycle. We're such a small fraction, actually, but like a swarm of locusts we're eating away at her lifetime after lifetime. These meditations are designed to help you identify the missing, misplaced, or misidentified puzzle pieces, and help you find your splinters. I use the word splinter because I think of something like heartbreak or jealousy as a splinter. A splinter, like a hangnail, gnaws on our psyche. Hurt gnaws. Grief gnaws. We know we don't like this, but we've come to live with these splinters as a part of ourselves. We have learned to live with lack. We have made it fit. But is lack really a truth or one of our many gnawing splinters?

Sometimes we come into our lives with the feelings we have. They are of us. We've carried them over from some other lifetime. Do we recognize these feelings and can we step away from them? That depends on our desire to acknowledge our hurt or stay in it. Sometimes I think we stay in hurt because it's what we know and find comfort in. If we know grief, for example, and continue to experience grief, we become absorbed in this emotional relationship to Earth as our own. Why wouldn't we embrace it? Grief has become a friend. But grief is killing the planet. It is our emotional nemesis. Grief pushes our minds to make decisions that will ultimately destroy this planet. Grief is a cancer, one we really need to begin to dismantle and heal from.

Grief is loss. It is the single most unbalanced energy on the planet. It is what topples nations. We are strong until we grieve. We're invincible until the roof comes crashing down around us. Some of us barrel through grief and pick up the pieces and push through it, but many of us stumble. We can't manage to continue. We're stuck. Broken. I have experienced the intense power of indecision when I have experienced grief. The emotional weight (and often grief appears silently as an unknown) of these experiences compounds the grief and destroys, like a cancer, clear thinking.

A nation grieving cannot think clearly and the people who rely on our leaders to steer us out of grief often flounder. Grief takes ahold of us all no matter our ethnicity or social standing. A nation grieving is a sinking barge until one of us, and then two of us, and then three and four of us resolutely stand firm. Call the grief out for what it is and begin a proactive approach to healing. We're a reactive species. Grief renders us incapable of coming together. We'll pit our emotions against one another and that self-destructive pattern will take hold until it takes us all down. We love grief because we love to hurt, to see others hurt. We love the stories of a rise and a fall. We love to falter and rise. Act and react. Taking proactive steps to change this mindset is possible. It takes a little more work that reacting, but if you're interested in taking a step forward and pulling yourself out of the seductive pattern of grief then I suggest you try a new approach to living.

I have to repeat this. We put ourselves in harm's way. We are attracted to hurt. I don't know all the reasons why we are, but throughout the years I've been working in this healing modality this is the invaluable insight I have gained. Hurt is our friend. Maybe it is because one day long, long ago when Earth hurt us we associated our experiences here as hurtful ones. After all, if a continent suddenly erupts or caves in we're going to react to this. Our ancestors would have taught us to fear Earth, and of course this has led to our fear of each other, but throughout these meditations I've been able to look at myself in relationship to the Earth's motion. A tsunami in Japan will be felt in the Americas and we will respond. We're animals. We're conditioned to flee or to fight if threatened. A tsunami in Japan will not reach us physically if we live across the globe, but the unseen bands of energy that the tsunami produces will be felt in our emotional body and we will react. We will say, "Earth is hurting us. She destroys. We must fight Earth. We must build up more walls. Fight." If we choose to flee we will do so aggrieved for all that we have lost and we will hurt.

Anger produces anger. My emotional body is in a relationship with Earth. My anger directs anger outwardly to be felt by others. Love is an antidote, we think, to this, but I've learned that a hurt is a hurt whether it be in light, in love, in anger, or despair. We love our hurt. And a hurt, in turn, will become attracted to us. The circle will continue over and over, lifetime after lifetime, until we pull out all the stops and correct the pattern.

I'm going to get some pushback on this. I'm prepared to defend my statements because as difficult as this is to grasp, it will be even more difficult to accept if you don't step into this with an open mind. We're attracted to hurt. To some, this will sound irresponsible and callous. "We're not attracted to hurt," you will say. "We're stuck in a socially downward spiral. This isn't my fault. I'm stuck in a job that doesn't pay well. I can't afford a new car. My baby needs medicine and you want me to believe you?" You will close the book and turn away because these words will hurt. But I will offer you one palm frond (a symbol of peace) in exchange for a conversation about this. You are where you are, and you can look at it as bad or you can look at it as possibly OK. I'm not asking you to compare your life to anyone else's. We're all in some form of pain. All of us. I may not struggle with money, but I sure as hell struggle to feel worthy, to feel I'm making a worthwhile contribution, to rise above the rejection and loneliness I experience, not only in my personal life, but in this writing career. I can either be here now and face this grief or I can turn away from it, continue to bury it under the rug only to feel it again and again until my emotionally drowning body is done. I choose not to drown, but to liberate myself from grief. I'm offering you a way forward and out from under the rug.

Money is and has always been perceived as the marker that defines our happiness. Money is the liberator, the panacea. Money is the root of all evil. Money is as money does. It is a tool. It is a chess piece. It is a band-aid. Money is what money is. We have it. We lose it. We're barred from it. We're swimming in it. There's not one of us not in a relationship with money. We either need it, need more of it, or live in some kind of emotional bubble within a sphere of ostentatiousness because this is our relationship to it and to the world. "Look what I can have," you might think. "What I am! Look!" We love to look, but then we throw stones. It's what we do. We hurt. We want others to hurt too. I will not offer you a way forward into money. If this is what you need more than anything right now might I suggest a different healing modality? I've read of many approaches where you visualize abundance, and in turn attract greater wealth, but this is not that kind of teaching. We're not going to visualize.

Together we're going to go in and clean out the emotional filing cabinet, sweep out from under the rug, and bring to the surface the fragments of the self that have been causing your grief. Then we're going to open these bulging files and either toss them or keep them. We're not going to tiptoe through the tulips and avoid anger or frustration. Our work will be more nuanced and ethereal, but then grounded in the knowledge that we are of Earth and must be on Earth to do this healing work. We'll then return from this healing experience with new insight and begin to see our planet in a new way.

It is extremely difficult for me to put myself into your shoes and vice versa; therefore, I will not even begin to try or ask you to do the same. I know what I know and you are what you are as a result of what you know and experience. I sympathize greatly, should you be in distress, but I can't feel what you feel, and for that I am sorry. I am being honest with you. I might feel something akin, or similar, but you are you and I am me. I hope you have one beautiful love of your life to cling to. I have my children. My friends. My self. I have the love of family. I have so much that pleases me and makes my heart sing. And I am grateful. In gratitude, I acknowledge all that is good. Over and over I turn my prayers to good. That which is good is a day off from work, a kind word, a well-paying job, intellectual curiosity. Generosity. That which is good is kindness. Friendship. Respect. I choose to look at what I want in return for what I give Earth. I choose acceptance, and in return receive acceptance because this is the energy I put out into the world.

The first thing I will ask you to do is write down three things that you are grateful for. I'll join you. I am grateful for the freedom to think without fear of being told I am wrong. I am grateful to live in a country where the freedom to communicate is possible. And I am grateful I have a fighting spirit to make things happen for myself rather than rely on someone else to do the work for me. These are broad, but effective and important criteria for me. I turn to these over and over. I am grateful for freedom, to live in a country where I can think and communicate without retaliation. I choose to communicate in an acceptable way, because if I threw bombs I might not get very far. So you get the idea. I am grateful I can see the country for what it is and use the system of accessible communication to my advantage. I choose not to fight with a gun or to lie in the street. I use the pen as my weapon. This is my tool. I am grateful words work. In gratitude, I work to find a way forward. I am me, but you are you. To be effective we just might need to fight, but let's first find some grace and do it in gratitude instead of retaliation because retaliation will just bring more retaliation; whereas, gratitude will return to us gratitude. We pull back in what we push out. Earth is a polarity and we are riding her waves.

Earth is a duality. She is hot as she is cold. She is force as she is grace. We are connected to the energies of Earth. We are emotionally teetering as though on a tilt-a-whirl because Earth tips. She tilts. We have no idea how deeply connected we are to the tilt. And why should we? Who has time to think about the relationship we have to the planet's magnetic push/pull? Maybe it has crossed your mind, or you have invested in deeply felt conversations with others about this very thing, but I'd like to open your mind to the idea that because Earth moves, we move. The wave is symbolic of the motion, and as much as this is a wave of water we see, it is as much the wave of energy we feel. This is the motion of the unseen cosmic waves. We are interrupted by these bands of energy, and because they displace us we become reactionary, but the more we grow to understand this relationship we're having, the more we can understand the responsibility we have to take care of our emotional/energetic body. And the more we learn to care for our self, the more we grow to understand the importance of taking care of the very being that makes us react. The more we treat Earth as a balanced, nuanced place, the more we will understand our own balanced, nuanced body.

The complications that arise as a result of imbalance are sickness, malaise, depression, and dare I say, mental illness. We are what we create. The desire to create a healthy lifestyle is paramount in many of us, but the only way to truly be healthy is to understand the relationship we have to the mind, and because the mind is in relationship to the planet, the two are interconnected. To give you an example, I'll share a personal story.

When I was unhappily married I don't think I truly understood how to be in a balanced relationship. Not only did I not understand the responsibility I had to my own happiness/unhappiness, for it was mine, I didn't understand how to communicate my desires to my former husband. I understood malaise, and I felt it, but because I couldn't get out from under that malaise I struggled to find even the good bits of the love that we shared. I saw only petty discomforts. I bought a lot of new clothes and went on expensive salon visits trying to find anything that would bring more pleasure than the discomfort of my relationship. I swept a lot under the rug. For years I went through the motions.

Motherhood was a blessed distraction, but the day our eldest daughter packed her bags and headed off to college I had that moment of reckoning. Who was I going to be now? My daughter was no longer going to need me in the same way and I panicked. Thinking about it now, I know I chose a divorce and a new beginning for myself rather than falling down into some emotional empty hole which would only result in me helicoptering my young adult children. Are we helicoptering our children because we don't trust the world? Or is it because we don't trust ourselves? Because we're lost? Frightened? Alone? Lonely?

This is just an observation, but should we let our children go without interfering in their lives as much as I am witnessing this interference, I do believe they will come out all right. I really do believe this. Are you afraid that your own children will be just as unsure of themselves as you are? Is this why you want to protect them and continue parenting them long after it is time to let them go? We're hurting and we're further hurting them and ourselves by holding onto them. Our greatest responsibility as parents is to witness our grown children. As difficult as this is to do (and I admit it is difficult not to invest in their landscape design), it is imperative we let our children discover their true selves and not impose our own version of that truth onto them.

I will be honest with you. I was pretty good at this, not perfect, but I recognized the importance of giving my daughters room to skin their knees (metaphorically speaking) in their budding young adult lives. Parenting them was my go-to. It came naturally, and I loved, and still do love being a mom as I try really hard to give both my daughters room to make their own discoveries. But on the day our eldest left for college I woke to the knowledge that I was truly unhappy. I had been looking within, but spending a lot of time looking at them. Suddenly, I was forced to look at the man I had been married to for over twenty years in a new way. Our youngest would be at this same crossroad in a few years and I realized that without her at home my husband and I would be looking at one another from across the table—just the two of us. Alone. I really did panic. I looked at all that dust that had been swept under the rug and flipped out. It was just too much to deal with. To not clean out your emotional filing cabinet is one of the largest burdens you will be left with. Unless you do it now you will return to another life after this one and do it all over again, potentially adding more weight, more dust, more unanswered files to your collected pile.

Throughout my meditations this is what I have seen. To clean out the emotional filing cabinet is the greatest gift you can give yourself, but because we don't want to do this, or even know that we should, let alone how to do it, we continue to let the dust collect, we let the files go unanswered, and we sweep it all away. But there will come that day when these emotional dust bunnies rear their ugly heads and you will be forced to address this fear of looking within. I walked out of my own experience wiser for it, but I feel compelled (compelled is an understatement), rather driven to help save you the burden of living year after year in a state of malaise. We don't have to. Cleaning isn't fun, but it is worth it when you can begin to see results. I can't promise you that you will love this, but what I can promise you is a greater appreciation for your own honesty. Sometimes all it takes is acknowledging that things are not what you'd like them to be. Then to acknowledge that you are responsible for the things not being what you like (because it is what your mind makes of them that makes them what they are), and then to realize the importance of cleaning.

I can just imagine the hairs on the back of your neck standing up. You're screaming, *no*! And now you close the book and toss it across the room. *Argh*! If you do have this reaction I applaud you for reading this far. If this is nothing you object to, and you're open to this idea, I invite you to continue.

VI

The Steps

I don't have a name for this healing modality. I was given a name, Healing With Isis, in a meditation fifteen years ago. I even bought the website domain name *healingwithisis.com*, but I never knew, and still don't know, how to use this name. I understand the ancient Egyptian mythology behind the name, but the name itself is now synonymous with terror. It is not a healing name.

By using the ancient Egyptian myth of the goddess Isis as a healing modality I am essentially taking the pieces of myself, discarding the ones that do not fit, and allowing myself a rebirth with the ones that do. I have been shown throughout these meditations that we can essentially rebirth ourselves without dying. We can take the pieces of the self, look at them carefully, and redesign ourselves more truthfully. To die is to prolong this. To die is cowardly. To die isn't some final act of glory. The idea is to eradicate our story self and get to the honesty within.

I am not a religious person. I could write a whole other book on this topic, but for now I will tell you that I am not coming to you with any preconceived notion of how to be good in the world based on a religious doctrine. Rather, I'm coming to you because my spirit, my simple, unadorned, uninterested-in-glory spirit is here to do a little soul work on myself. I've chosen to share this idea with you because I feel driven to do so. This is not a religious document. I'm not asking you to follow me, but to follow yourself to heal yourself to then share yourself. If you've been given this book then I'm glad it was a gift. If you bought this book please know that your money is appreciated. I'm glad that we have had this exchange.

These are the words of my soul. My soul self has spent countless hours recording and studying this ancient Egyptian modality of healing. For me it has become a truth. I am not afraid of the meditations. They are a lot of work, but I've seen results.

I'm learning to balance, to stand on the tippy top of a needle looking down on two sides: the left and the right, the right and the wrong, the dark and the light, the good and the bad, the this and the that. This needle is tippy. I can't stand up here for long without shaking. I am trying to find balance in this dualistic world of yes and no, of hot and cold, of truth and lies. I am here. I am not there. My here is my now. I live to be here now. I live to rejoice in life instead of being ashamed, guilty, frustrated, jealous, or heartbroken by it. I live to rejoice now. I am not looking to go anywhere else where it is perceived to be better. It just is. And I am centering myself to observe.

Do I need a marketing plan or a name for this healing modality? Probably. Would you respect Healing With Isis? Probably not. Isis is no longer a name I think any of us wants to associate with, because it now refers to a terrorist group. I could easily write another chapter on this phenomenon: Earth (and, as a result, her people) churns out opposition. This is why we encounter defeat each and every time we try goodness. Goodness will always get pushback, but how we see, feel, and react to the pushback becomes our relationship to goodness. I experienced frustration, resentment, rejection, and disappointment as ISIS emerged and took away any chance I had of using this name, but rather than throw in the towel, because I felt defeated, I decided to push back at evil and find a new way to introduce the healing program. Essentially, I tore up the script. I took out what no longer fit and reworked the bits that were still sound, but I worked hard finding new ways to conceptualize the healing. By not calling this program Healing With Isis, I hope I have come forward into greater truth. I know I have taken a bigger step toward openness and inclusivity.

Isis was once known a mythological deity. She was seen as a goddess figure. She was probably pagan. At least she became pagan, a word we use to differentiate from religious. Isis was a mother, she was associated with rebirth, and she was worshipped as the giver of life, but over time she became an unacceptable religious figure. *Because* she was a woman? No. She was once celebrated because she was a woman. Isis was sexual and she was adored. She was seen as the creator goddess, a co-creator with Osiris, part of the creation story. She was a woman. Have I said this? I have. And I must say it again to make a point. Women, in all their fullness, their completeness, were at one time celebrated in our religions. Mother Mary, the Christian figure, was a woman. She was a mother, but she was a virgin. Or so the story goes. We like our stories. We like our goddesses, our religious icons, our figures, but they are versions of ourselves in story. Isis was a way of thinking. We designed her. We continue to design her. Mother Mary is a design. We like our women to be virtuous, but it's a tall order to have a baby without having intercourse. Is it even possible? Not for the average Eve.

So where does this leave women? Without a role model. Religions are faltering around the globe. Mothers in all parts of the world are in an intense moment of reckoning. Who are we? Some religious ideal? Saints? No. We're working doubly hard in 2021 during a worldwide pandemic to put food on the table for our families, educate our children, and hold it together. We have lost our jobs. We don't have time to work on ourselves. There's immense truth to this statement. There are many mothers who simply do not have time for this discussion. I want to recognize them. I respect you magnificently, but I encourage you to step away from feeling like you have to do it all. Your children should be doing more. For balance.

I will admit that it is easier for me to stand on top of the needle at this stage of my life and look down on this situation, but I was once in the midst of my own emotional pandemic. I understand. I have stepped away from the physicality of motherhood, the push/pull of my ego, the need to be best, to be right, to hold my children accountable, to prove my worthiness above all else, but I remember it well. I can now look down on it objectively and I want to help. Isis is a way of thinking. We have at one time circled toward her and worshiped Earth, but have now gone far afield to other horizons. Earth teaches us her stories, but then we rewrite them over and over. I'll call this healing modality healing with the goddess. It is a healing with the self. We are our own goddess, our own Isis, our own rebirth.

Healing with our self brings us to the self. Do we like this self? That depends on your relationship to yourself. Are you OK spending time with yourself? Are you prepared to get to know you? Healing requires introspection. Dealing with the day-to-day requires juggling. Going inward frees you up from juggling in the long run, but until you trust yourself you won't find this freedom. Freedom might look like a night off from homework and baths. It becomes a glass of wine. Freedoms like these are shortened by the knowledge that tomorrow will be more of the same, but by changing your outlook on the day-to-day you can shift the way the day-to-day controls you.

One of the first things I ever did when beginning to meditate as an adult was remember my childhood. My Quaker upbringing helped me forge a beginning relationship to meditation that, at the time, I didn't foresee or really appreciate. Meeting, as it is called in the Society of Friends, is difficult for a child to sit through, but my mother (thank you again, Mom) never doubted that my younger brother and I could. I don't remember questioning the painful forty minutes of silence we were asked to sit in, after all I was a child who didn't question (I was a pretty agreeable, quiet child), but we probably begged to leave the meditation service every single Sunday that we went to

Hopewell Friends Meeting. I do remember wanting to run around the lawn, play in the rotting carriage shed, or explore the graveyard while sitting there staring out the large paned windows. I have nine generations of ancestors buried in that graveyard. It's a lovely little graveyard shaded with large trees and enclosed behind crumbling limestone walls. As children we looked for our relatives on the worn markers.

I remember swinging my legs on the tippy old wooden meeting house bench while fidgeting in the acute silence, but Mom would put her hand on my knee and look down at me. She didn't have to say anything in that moment. I knew what she meant. As she explained it to me, and of course to my younger brother, our movements jolted the whole bench which then rocked on the old wooden floor, and disturbed everyone else. This hand on my knee was the signal to stop fidgeting. I think of this now as a metaphor for my life. I have learned to appreciate the notion of not causing unease or unhappiness for anyone else, but at the same time I recognize the difficulty of doing so. It is easy to not think of others, but to think only of ourselves as we advocate ferociously for ourselves. Once again, I encourage a way forward that supports looking out for others on this tippy Earth as we advocate for greater freedoms within.

The limestone meeting house, built in the late 1780's, sits adjacent to a cattle farm, and in the summer the flies come into the building through the large, open, insufficiently screened windows. When they landed on our arms, or legs, or the top of our heads, my brother and I would play this game with ourselves to see how long we could stand the prick of their creepy little legs on our perspiring skin until we felt the desperate urge to swat them away. Why weren't we given the paper fans? That would have done the trick. But alas, no fans for us. We were asked to sit still and contemplate the meaning of God as we watched the flies turn slowly and stealthily in circles exploring our skin. My relationship to God began as one of curiosity, of acceptance. I felt secure in a place, a space, and in the awareness that my grandparents, my great-grandparents, my great-great-grandparents, etc. once sat on those same benches feeling the creepy prick of flies' legs on their skin while learning to appreciate their Divine Awareness through meditation.

As I mentioned, I never foresaw myself teaching meditation, but I did have a foundation for it early on in my young life. I'm grateful for the lesson in stillness as I have taken this experience with me all of my life. Stillness is an important part of these meditations. I imagine some of you will do them while walking the dog, or practicing yoga, and I would never tell you not to; after all, I am encouraging you to find your own way through this with my help. But the discipline of sitting in silence and taking yourself down into the heart of the Earth to connect to your higher self is about the mindfulness of the moment. It is not about doing anything else. The healing comes through the stillness of the moment. It comes because you're learning a new discipline that will help you engage with your true self.

To help you get started on this path to mindful meditation I offer the following steps:

Step One: Acknowledge the difficulty of _____.

Step Two: Admit you're ready to do something about this difficulty.

Step Three: Acknowledge that the difficulty is

only a difficulty because this is how you see it. Acknowledge that your mind sees it as a difficulty.

Step Four: Admit that the difficulty is a personal difficulty. It might belong to others, be a universal difficulty, but for all practical purposes it is yours alone because you see it, thus making it yours, an individual difficulty.

Step Five: Write this difficulty down on a piece of paper.

Step Six: Write down a reasonable time you're willing to give to yourself each day to meditate on this difficulty. I would like to recommend ten minutes a day. Meditation is not looking at the TV or listening to the radio when you have a spare ten minutes. Meditation is eyes closed. No phone. Ask your children to meditate with you. This can be a family affair.

Step Seven: Record your thoughts. Write down what comes to you in each meditation session. For example: *I need to take the chicken out of the freezer.* Write it down. *I need to stop calling my mom every day. It's draining me. She's terribly insecure. We need a new phone schedule.* Write it down. *The dog is barking again at the neighbors.* Write it down. By getting in the habit of acknowledging you, the all of you, the all of you will begin to have a voice.

Step Eight: Continue writing down your creative ideas/thoughts/musings/complaints/admissions. You're not being asked to do anything with these. Not yet. Just record them. If you prefer to do this as voice memos then by all means do so, but I personally think it's easier to go back and look at yourself on paper than through a series of recordings.

Step Nine: Give yourself one month before reading your words then read them without commentary. Just read them. They are you. You don't have to praise yourself or criticize yourself. Try neutrality. Highlight one or two observations that stick out. For example: *I need to spend less money on shoes.* Or: *I should stop doing my husband's laundry.* Or: *I need a new yoga mat. I deserve it.* Or: *Homeschooling during a worldwide pandemic is extremely difficult. I have zero patience.* Or: *I'm an awesome lover.* Or: *I love knitting.* Only highlight one or two. This will be difficult to do, as you will have a lot of thoughts that have meaning, but highlight accordingly.

Step Ten: Write down the one or two thoughts that you have chosen as most relevant and put them in the sentence I have provided in Step One. For example: *Acknowledge the difficulty of <u>love</u>.* Perhaps your sentence would then read: *I acknowledge the difficulty of (self) love because I feel guilty when I buy new shoes. I acknowledge the difficulty of love because my husband refuses to do his own laundry and I just end up resenting him. I acknowledge the difficulty of (self) love because I don't feel I deserve a new yoga mat. I acknowledge the difficulty of love because I'm a terrible mother with zero patience. I acknowledge the difficulty of love because I'm an awesome lover but my boyfriend prefers to spend time with his friends. I acknowledge the difficulty of (self) love because I love to knit, but I don't spend enough time doing the things I love to do.* By acknowledging, you bring awareness and voice to the difficulty.

There is nothing bad or wrong with having a difficulty, or many, for that matter. They exist. By giving difficulty a place to be, to acknowledge something as a difficulty, we honor the unswept carpet, the bulging filing cabinet, the abandoned stone well where we have buried these emotions. I use these images as examples. Please feel free to use your own visual if these don't work for you, but the idea that we sweep emotions under the rug, file away our feelings, or dump the mother lode of our unhappiness into our emotional well where it sits for years collecting dirt and grime and becoming this gross kind of sludge, is my way of offering explanation. I want to acknowledge, alongside you, that we build walls. We refuse to deal with emotions. We resort to wine and shopping. We need more to life than coping. We need solutions.

I am not a licensed psychologist or therapist. I am a Reiki Master of Masters turned novelist, essayist, and poet. Are these credentials you trust? I don't know. Only you can answer this. My evolution of my self has been trying to figure out how to put the work I do into language where more people can benefit from helping themselves. This is not to upend an industry. One is not better than the other. There is everything right about therapy just as there is everything right about meditation. As long as we get to ourselves without turning away from the very aspect of ourselves that gives us the answers, we'll be fine, but too many of us turn away from ourselves. We're frightened. We're truly frightened of what we will find. I'd like to simplify the process and give you a place to go where you don't have to fight with yourself to discover yourself. Meditation can become your friend. It is not scary.

Now that you have completed the first ten steps of this exercise and you have written a sentence or two outlining your difficulty, I'd like to invite you to meditate on the sentence. You will now spend ten minutes a day on the sentence. And, yes, your mind will wander. You'll think about everything but the sentence because you won't like this, but that's OK. Trust yourself with yourself. Be your own best friend. This is your thought so own it. Own the words: I am having difficulty with _____.

I'll do this exercise with you because occasionally I still struggle with rejection. My sentence is: I acknowledge the difficulty of <u>rejection</u>. I acknowledge feeling rejection even when it is not the intention of someone to reject me, but because I struggle with rejection I assume they are out to hurt me. I respond in a panic. I assault. I cry. I get angry. I hurt. I close myself down and wallow. I do all or some of the above.

Over the years there has been a lot less hurt and I no longer need to do this particular exercise all that often, but on the occasion when rejection still jabs at me I will acknowledge that this wound runs deep. I try really hard not to blame someone else for the rejection I feel, but to ask for clarification. I will ask for their intention behind the comment. I will then ask for further clarification and explanation if need be. I will admit to wallowing, pouting, and calling a friend who will lend a helpful, loving ear, but I don't blame. The rejection is mine to feel. It is not a loved one's or a literary agent's intention to lance my heart.

I once thought I'd solved the problem for myself by creating a steel cage around my heart to protect myself from rejection, but then over and over the steel cage would get ripped off in some meditation and I'd be forced to look at the wound anew. Band-aids won't work in this healing program. You will be asked to pull out old sutures, oftentimes let the wound bleed again so that you can clean it out properly, and then let it rest. You will be able to look at the pieces of shrapnel you have dislodged and toss them for good when you are ready to do so. Remember, we love our grief. It's an aphrodisiac. It is what we know. We love to hurt as much as we love to see others hurt. We love to help, but we love to hurt. We're a polarity. Stand on top of the needle looking down on it all and notice yourself as much a grieving individual as a happy-go-lucky individual. You'll learn to balance the two. We're never just one way. We're nuanced, complicated, troubled, and creative problem-solving individuals. We're uniquely our own.

Step Eleven: Continue to meditate on your sentence. Give yourself an unspecified amount of time to do this. I encourage you to tuck this sentence into your heart as you enjoy each of the free meditations I offer on my website. These meditations are there to help you get started, to remind you of your own true self, and to take you along on a journey that, for me, has been highly rewarding. I am ready to share. I encourage you to use your sentence as a jumping-off point so that if you join the meditation series, or even if you don't, you can use it to help set an intention for the meditation. Sometimes other things will come up in the meditation that you will feel compelled to address, but I encourage you to give this time. It will not always be fun, but it will be empowering. Your words matter. Your words will heal. Your thoughts matter. Your thoughts will heal.

I can't promise you that slap-to-the-forehead moment of healing proclamation. Does that really exist? I guess it does if you can make your mind believe that it does, but that takes some mighty strong convictions. I don't own that kind of trust in the universe. This kind of trust, to me, is wayward and built on the premise of God and hope. I don't want to wait and hope for God to heal me. I want God's worth to come through me. I am my own creative light, capable of creative construction, knowledge, harmony, and balance. I take responsibility for myself. God is a vocabulary word for most of us, and God wears many hats, but God, to me, is me. I am a fraction of God. I am part of the whole. I am my own creativity having been created. I am my own creator continually creating.

The body of this healing work is and will always be thought-based. I am fortunate that I do not struggle with disease or lingering health issues. I cannot write this book having successfully come through a bout of cancer. This is not my experience. My experience is psychological, but if I'm not careful with my thoughts this could lead to a serious psychosomatic health issue, because, as we know, the mind and the body are one. I could very easily talk myself into a heart issue if I failed to heal my (perceived) wounded heart. I am my own creativity. I am my own mind. I am my own demise if I'm not careful. I am my own best healer.

I will encourage you to find a friend, a mother, a father, a husband, a psychologist, counselor, or priest to help you when you're feeling down. We need these people in our lives to help make that teetering moment of trying to stay balanced, seen. I feel these witnesses are important. We require their eyes on us so that we can begin to recognize ourselves. I am learning to balance my own insight with the insight of others. We're all here to witness and be witness to the Earth experience. Balance requires a lot of stability. Loved ones, friends, and licensed professionals can help us with this process so I encourage you to share your meditation experiences with someone who will listen and not judge you. Some of this will be remarkably private and only for you, but you'll be surprised how easily the sharing will come once you fall in love with yourself. How can you throw yourself under the bus for not being as pulled together as you'd like to be if you love yourself? You can't. You will owe yourself forgiveness and truth. This is love.

Step Twelve: Share as you can and feel it is appropriate to do so. Do you share that you've had a bungled affair with your boss and you're trying to work through the hurt? I can't answer that. Maybe there is someone in your life you can share this with. Maybe not. Maybe the bungled affair is part of a larger unrecognized pattern of self-destructive behavior that only manifested itself in an affair. Maybe there is something else related to this behavior you are working through that is shareable? Do you share that your daughter is struggling with bulimia? Only if you can. Only with your daughter's permission. Only when you recognize you might be the one who has control issues that need addressing because your need to control is a household issue. She is of you and what you teach. I'm not suggesting that you become a wide-open book to be scrutinized by all. I'm merely suggesting that, in time, and in the manner that is best, you share your difficulties.

They are who you are. Be seen for this. It's a level of vulnerability that gives you voice. It makes you real.

Steps One through Twelve are complete. This is not a slam dunk nor is this book intended to become a substitute for more traditional therapies. It is one aspect of a healing modality to teach you the importance of self-care. We're responsible for ourselves. We have to stop waiting to be cared for. It's killing us. Look within our communities. More and more people need help. My heart goes out to them. They need jobs. Housing. Clothing. Education. Equal rights. Voting rights. Citizenship. We need to help them reach a level of dignity and help them regain their footing. We can teach self-care through public awareness and universal health programs. It is a universal truth that we want to blame others for our problems. We want to push away the hurt. We want. We need. All this want and all this need is toppling our nation and our psyches, but the answer doesn't lie in a Democratic program or a Republican program. It lies in a balanced program.

The founding intention behind the creation of the United States government was to balance the thinking of two parties. One was not supposed to be better. One was not supposed to be right. The two-party system was designed and therefore recognized to be in deliberate opposition, throwing one thought against the other (because our Founding Fathers recognized plurality). We've come a long way from the very sophisticated, nuanced thinking that went into the foundation of the United States government. We've swamped that boat by amending the U.S. Constitution because, as with all things, we can interpret, reinterpret, and craft images and ideas for as long as we're able. This can be seen as a fantastic thing because by doing so we are addressing racial inequality, women's rights, voting rights, and gender rights, but because we are a plurality not one person or group will succeed without opposition. We must also recognize the distinct harm we are doing by playacting control. By continually chipping away at the essence of the U.S. Constitution, our governing bodies can ratify amendments, shift the Supreme Court, and create loopholes such as the filibuster (something our Founding Fathers never foresaw), essentially crippling the Senate. By pushing up against our foundation and jostling the nuance of the United States' two-party system, we're challenging democracy. Is this something we really want to do? We're capable of destruction just as we're capable of repair. We like our stories. We like to hurt. I'd like to offer this: nuance is not an either/or. It is not right or wrong. Nuance is taking all that is best and discerning it for the good of the whole. Greed is a vice. Greed hurts. Greed is not healthy. Greed wounds the self and our true selves suffer.

By crafting a relationship to the self we become less dependent on others and more reliant on the self. It takes a lot of courage to stop tipping one way and then the other. It takes insight to stand firm on that needle and look down at the swirling currents of inequality, but it takes action within to heal the hurt, the jealousy, the indignation, the greed, and the expectation. I can't teach you how you're going to help yourself. I'm offering you a way forward to start you on a path toward awareness. We're responsible for ourselves, but we need to trust ourselves. We need to trust that the planet is a safe place and then we can begin to trust. Period.

In conclusion, I'd just like to say that this idea

of balance is a way. It is a way out of hurt and into healing. Isis was a symbolic Egyptian goddess figure who put the pieces of her mate, Osiris (Ruler of All Living Things) back together after he had been hacked to death by his brother in a jealous fit. Isis took the pieces, the fractions, and together with her sister Nephthys repaired Osiris's body so that he would live forever as Ruler of the Dead. Isis is the healer. She is the repairer. Osiris has not died, but lives to rule for eternity. Healing with Isis becomes a way of looking at the pieces of yourself, honoring them, and rearranging them, if need be, to put yourself right. It is a rebirth, but you don't have to die to become whole and Earth can become your heaven. As I have mentioned, I have fought with the idea of crafting a healing modality and calling it Healing With Isis. Fifteen years ago it was a doable idea. I understood then that I was coming through an initiation, and to this day I recognize that my initiation into the world of the fractured self has brought me to you. But I have thrown away the script. I have torn up my past. I have re-created image, old thinking, and pushed past fears and insecurities. At the heart of this experience I have redesigned myself as myself, but I am not the same quiet little girl. I am no longer afraid of the teacher. I have something to offer.

After much consideration and internal debate I have come to the conclusion that I cannot call this healing modality Healing With Isis. Healing With Isis represents the past. This is the Now. But my Now is of the past, the present, and it will be of the future. My Now, this landscape design, consists of multiple puzzle pieces, some discarded, and many newly found. My Now is seeped in the knowledge that women were once celebrated and adored as co-creators on this planet, and my Now is full in the knowledge that women will one again embark on their own self-healing journey toward greater beauty and acceptance. As we move forward, begin to craft our images, and come into our own Now moments, it is time we stop the blame game and return to our inner truths, our inner well of happiness, love of others, and most importantly, the love of self. There will be a name for this healing, but it will be your own.

Please visit *aliciacahalanelewis.com/meditations* for more on the meditation series. There you will find more of a specific program to follow. The meditations were written and recorded by me, and you will be guided by my voice throughout. Your mind will wander, but don't worry. Simply steady your breath and return to the sound of my voice. You will think you do not have time to do these, but I encourage you to make the time. They are simple to follow and easy to come in and out from. Your children can follow along or draw pictures alongside you as you listen. Make this a time without electronics. I have nothing against electronics, because electronics are useful tools, and you will need a computer or a tablet to listen to the meditations, but our children need balance too. Teach them at a young age to sit in silence so that their minds will wander. Maybe they, too, will learn to watch a fly crawl on their skin without reacting. Let's teach our children to find their own creativity, peace, and a restful place to land.

I encourage you to begin the meditation series in the month you find yourself ready to begin. If you're reading this book in July pick up the series there. If you're reading this in November, pick it up there. You will find the meditations are labeled Winter into Spring, Spring into Summer, Summer into Fall, and Fall into Winter. You will begin at your own starting point and return to that starting point. Begin at your own beginning.

My heart is open to what I am discovering about myself, but this is because I am no longer afraid of what I might find. I was once a troubled little girl loved and loving, but who was missing some huge piece of her puzzle. She was numbed by an unspecified "loss," yet was unsure what it was that was missing. I have been lost, but now I am found. I never thought I would become a meditation teacher, but by working through the sludge, sorting the pieces, and rearranging the daughter/wife/mother/writer/lover/Reiki Master/healer/teacher into a more truthful arrangement, I can share with you that my landscape puzzle is authentic. I have drawn on the knowledge of the saints and the archangels, the true masters of healing, compassion, and love. I feel attuned to them as they have been my guides throughout this initiation. I encourage you to listen too. It is the greatest gift we can give ourselves.

Author's Note

I would like to extend a personal invitation to you to reach out to me via my website at *aliciacahalanelewis.com* and send me a message if you would like further assistance with this meditation series. I can be reached through the email link on the site and will gladly offer assistance to individuals and/or small groups of two to three persons should you need further explanation or help getting started. All of this work comes from my own personal truth, my own insight. I have been working alongside The Galactic Council, Archangel Michael, Archangel Raphael, Mother Mary, Mary Magdalene, Isis, Thoth, and Guan Yin for over twenty years. I am not a simple person, nor am I complex. I'm a straight shooter when it comes to sharing.

We are manifesting a life on one plane of existence, our Earth, but it is an illusion. This Earth is never ours unless we make it the way we want it to be. If we think of Earth as a destructive plane of existence it will be so. If we deem it a loving plane of existence this is what we will experience. Our insights create. The illusion gets created when we think that our own thoughts don't matter. This is not true.

I could have written extensively about our relationship to the Covid-19 virus, because at the time of this writing we are in the midst of a pandemic, but I chose not to. This isn't because I don't know what to say about it, but because the worldwide coronavirus pandemic is incomplete. There is more to experience. We are on the cusp of a sea change, a re-set, and the virus is a disrupter. How we respond to a disrupter is how we respond. Do we respond in fear and let a virus control us or do we work alongside the virus and live in coexistence? Fear is dominating the relationship we have to the planet so of course many of us are in fear. Many of us are in denial. Many of us are lost in thoughts that are not our own. I encourage you to distance yourself from fear. Try not to fear the virus. Do not fear the vaccine. We will have this particular virus with us for a long time. It will mutate again and again. As a disrupter, the virus acts as a killing machine, but more than a killing machine it acts as a catalyst for change. If this idea resonates with you will you be able to look at a disrupter in a new way? In what way can a disrupter become a provider? What good can come from these opportunities that offer a re-set?

Living in balance with a disrupter such as a virus, or a sister-in-law, or a politician, or a dictator, or the tech giant who is sucking the very life out of us, is a difficult and trying part of our life here on Earth. These are not equal disrupters, by the way, but examples of what we live with on our journey to personal freedom. The United States will repeatedly get tested, as will most of the world. How we recognize opposition, how we work with opposition, and how we dismantle fear and reconstruct the story will be how we fail or succeed as we're continuously pushed up against a disrupter.

I don't know what the answers are. I don't have a crystal ball to see into the future, but what I do see is this: We're incomplete human beings on a journey to understand and accept Earth as a living microcosm of duality. Earth is a complex matrix of some of the more advanced energetic matrices in the universe. It is not just one plane, although this is what we see, but several complicated planes of duality. Sometimes these planes of duality fold in on themselves and become quadruple planes of existence, and when they fold again they become octagonal in form. The matrix is ever evolving, making it really complicated to be here. Time becomes irrelevant, but we fight to make it relevant. Space becomes irrelevant, but we demand that it, too, become relevant.

Imagine trying to stand on the tip of a needle in a hurricane. Of course you're going to lose your balance. Not once, but often. By learning to balance through meditation you can begin to balance your journey here. Meditation isn't for everyone, but should you come to the end of this little book and find yourself intrigued, curious, willing to give it a go, I encourage you to acknowledge the difficulty I asked you to write down and meditate on, as a disrupter. Start there. I wish you all my best on your journey as you begin to balance disruption with the joy you expect.

In love and gratitude,
Alicia

Acknowledgments

I am deeply grateful to so many loved ones from various lifelong spiritual guides and teachers, including my parents, to my grandparents, to college roommates, to best friends, and to partners and companions for their unique, loving, and yes, jostling contributions to my life.

I am humbled by my daughters, Sarah and Lydia, their insight, strength, and inner vision. May they, and their spouses, Adrian and Adam, whom I so adore, be blessed with ample opportunities to love and parent their own children, and may that love be returned to them in spades. This love is the greatest gift we can give one another.

I am most especially grateful to Marsha Stultz at Evolve Inc. who, for over eighteen years, has been a friend/teacher/contributor/witness to my evolution. I am grateful to Winslow McCagg who seems to know, unequivocally and without hesitation, that the personal freedoms we agonize about and endlessly search for lie within. More than a teacher, more than a dear friend, he is an inspiration.

To J'Lyn Chapman and Maureen Owen at Naropa University, thank you for seeing me. Really seeing me. Thank you Amanda Ngoho Reavey, Joseph Braun, Linda Quennec, and Ginger Teppner for your invaluable and continued support.

A heartfelt thank you to Mindy Ray, Dawn Omo, Madi

Omo, Tiernan Ryden and Dave Ferruolo. Their commitment to self-love, self-awareness, and self-healing encouraged me to pursue this career.

A generous thank you to Lee Bumsted for putting her eagle eye on this manuscript and helping to make it ready for publication. In that vein, my sincerest thank you to Emily Kallick at Wildember Marketing for making all my social media phobias go away with the wave of her magic wand. Yes, she really does have one for this job. I am indebted to her and her vision for making this book real, for her technological savvy and know-how in the meditation series recordings, and for her invaluable help putting these pieces of myself out into the world.

Should this little book find itself in your hands, I will be eternally grateful to you if you would share it with others. The relationship you will have with meditation will be your own. The relationship you will have with the planet and with your angelic guidance will be your own. Thank your guides who are celebrating alongside you for the opportunity to be here. Now. The gift of life is far more beautiful than we're willing to accept. This gift of life with all its irregularities is the nuance we seek.

www.ingramcontent.com/pod-product-compliance
Lightning Source LLC
Chambersburg PA
CBHW072210100526
44589CB00015B/2470